Patrick Dalzel Job

D1550121

THE MOUNTAINS WAIT

THEODOR BROCH

Inset. A PASS ISSUED BY THE GERMANS:
"The holder of this permit, the Mayor of Narvik, has permission to be on the streets of Narvik day or night."

THEODOR BROCH

★

THE MOUNTAINS WAIT

With an Introduction by

His Excellency The
PRIME MINISTER OF NORWAY

ILLUSTRATED BY
ROCKWELL KENT

MICHAEL JOSEPH LTD.
26 Bloomsbury Street, London, W.C.1

FIRST PUBLISHED MAY 1943
SECOND IMPRESSION MAY 1943
THIRD IMPRESSION MAY 1944

Set and printed in Great Britain by Unwin Brothers Ltd.,
at the Gresham Press, Woking, in Bembo type,
eleven point, leaded, and bound by James Burn.

Introduction

THE town of Narvik grew up with the coming of the Industrial Revolution to Norway. We had our industrial revolution late, when the age of electricity set free the latent power of Norway's abundant "white coal." Yet it was not so much electricity as the construction of the iron ore railway from Kiruna in Sweden which transformed Narvik in the space of a generation from a tiny little trading post into a modern worktown of nearly 10,000 souls. The railway brought work and money and happiness—and also a multitude of problems—to this far northern community. When Theodor Broch arrived at Narvik in 1930 as a young lawyer fresh from his studies in Oslo he found a lively, active community of railwaymen, dockers, townsfolk, farmers and fishermen grappling with their local problems in the typical democratic Norwegian way. Within four years he found himself in the midst of Narvik's public affairs—as its mayor. For another six years he helped his fellow-citizens to govern themselves by our well-tried methods of free discussion and co-operative endeavour, and then the wide world suddenly struck Narvik with that shattering impact which woke us all from our long dream of peace.

Narvik's iron ore traffic, its rail link with Sweden, and its harbour facilities had become the object of Germany's military ambitions. How Theodor Broch and his fellow-citizens faced up to the tremendous new tasks with which they were confronted is told in the pages of this book. It is the story of the Narvik Campaign, with its dramatic naval battles and its defeat of the German land forces, told from the inside by one who stayed at his post of civilian duty throughout the whole two months of incessant strain and trial. At the same time it is much more than the story of a campaign. By describing the human background of the military conflict, by portraying in vivid sketches the life of the ordinary people and the way they tackled their common problems in peace as well as in war, Theodor Broch has really told the essential story of our Norwegian democracy's struggle to perfect itself, and when threatened by the Nazi aggressors, to preserve itself against all assaults.

I hope that, with the help of this book, English readers will gain a closer understanding of our way of life, which in many respects is so like their own, and will be better able to appreciate the causes which lie behind the great struggle which is being conducted by our Home Front to-day —a struggle for freedom and democracy and the moral values of civilized society.

Johan Nygaardsvold

Prime Minister of Norway

LONDON

Contents

List of Illustrations

Narvik

I

THE mountains had closed behind us. After a night of strenuous climbing we had reached the plains between the snow-capped peaks and the last of winter ice slowly melting in the shadows behind them. The Laplander boy who was guiding me through the mountains to Sweden said we could take a breath now. There was no longer any danger of being overtaken.

We had come from a ravaged and looted land. We had seen our country invaded and occupied by hordes of men in green uniforms. The last front in northern Norway where the Germans had suffered their first defeat of the war had been given up. Narvik had been evacuated by the British and our other Allied friends. They were on their way to France to try to stop the deluge before the gates of Paris. We had left behind burning cities and a confused people.

Three days before from Harstad, a little town on Norway's largest island, our little family of three, the youngest lady three years old, had sailed into the fjords in a small craft manned by an old fisherman and his young son. I was being sought by the Germans throughout northern Norway. The sheriffs of the district and the German patrols had been ordered to return me to Narvik. I was said to be a British spy.

As Mayor of occupied Narvik, I had negotiated with the Germans. We had not always agreed too well. I had sent information to the British warships, and their heavy guns had silenced the German positions. Norwegian and Allied troops had recaptured the city and had held it for a week, but had been forced to give it up. Now the Germans were in control of all Norway.

In a little cabin deep in a fjord arm near the Swedish border I had been forced to leave my wife and daughter with friends, and to go on alone with a Lap guide into the mountains toward Sweden.

Now we stood beside a cairn on a mountain crag. The cairn marked the Swedish border. We threw down our knapsacks and took a brief rest.

Before going on I looked for a long time on what I could yet see of Norway. The ocean was no longer visible. Mountains stretched on all sides, with snow and green moss scattered between. Mountain streams shone like silver ribbons. The lakes were open, but ice bordered the shores. The wild heather had already coloured its small, hard flowers, and but for them the dominating tone was grey.

It was a harsh land we had, but never had it been so delightful, so desirable as now. Our leading men had already been driven abroad. Our ships had been sunk or had sailed away. All along the border were young men like myself. Thousands more would follow. We had to leave to learn the one craft we had neglected.

We had built good homes in the mountains, but we had neglected to fence them properly. Now strangers had taken over our land. They would loot and pluck it clean before we returned. But the country itself they could not spoil. The sea and the fjords and the mountains—to these we alone could give life. We were coming back. The mountains would wait for us.

Now the summer would come to the Northland but I would not be there. It was June, 1940.

I remembered that it was almost ten years to the day since we—Ellen and I—had come up here to build a life together. The time had passed rapidly, although much had happened in these years. It was in June that we had arrived, June, 1930.

We came from friendships and restaurants, from student debates on Freud and Marx and resolutions proposing the reform of the world. I was a young lawyer, she was a young housewife, without too much house-keeping to do. We came from great dreams, and difficulties with the rent. We came from the nation's Capital.

Two days before, in Oslo, we had taken the train for Narvik through Sweden. We could have taken a train to Trondheim and a steamer from there up the coast, but it would have been more expensive and we would not have had the trip abroad. Now we were approaching our destination. The train had worked its way up along evenly-climbing slopes on the Swedish side of the border. Already, through a cleft in the mountain below us, we could see the distant blue-green ocean. Down there lay Narvik.

The last mile or two we sat in silence looking down upon the fjord.

The scene came and went in panorama as the many tunnels opened the way for the train on its steep and winding road. Coming out of the last tunnel, we saw the whole town in sharp focus as if it lay under a magnifying glass. Even so, it was smaller than I imagined.

"Could anything ever happen in such a sleepy little town?"—I mused aloud.

"It certainly is a beautiful town," Ellen said encouragingly, "and at least it is smiling in its sleep."

To us the trip was more than an excursion. We had come to stay, to build a home and a law practice in a young and vigorous country. Here, I had thought, a young lawyer would not have to lick stamps for ten years before being permitted to write the letter itself. But now I was not so sure. A silent anxiety crept over me at the thought of beginning a new life.

I wondered if my imagination had created a fairyland.

True, our conquest of Narvik was disguised under the pretext of a summer visit to my parents, who had arrived the previous autumn. This arrangement somewhat reduced both the glory and the risk of our adventure. My father was Colonel of the Northern Hålogoland Regiment with headquarters in Narvik. In a year or two he might be ordered south again, if he should survive and a colleague down south should not.

There were still remnants of winter in the mountains, but down by the fjord the birches welcomed us in a veil of new, light-green spring. As we stepped off the train the Station Master came towards us without his overcoat, as though in demonstration of the fact that the tourist season was about to begin.

Although we knew that we were more than welcome, we wanted to take as little advantage of the Colonel as possible and rather specialize on the parents. And there on the station platform they were, Father in uniform, Mother in a new hat.

A taxi brought us across the town to the Regimental Headquarters on the hill not far from the white-framed City Hospital.

The welcome was everywhere evident—in the vases of flowers in the guest room, in the silver coffeepot gleaming on the table in the living-room downstairs, in my favourite cookies, prepared in abundance. For the first time in many years I was going to live at home.

Like many students from conservative environments, I felt it my duty during my University years to revolt against tradition and old-fashioned ideas. I had lived alone on the wrong side of the town and supported myself by selling advertising for magazines of poor circulation.

As the days passed we were introduced to the quiet little town. The introduction was made with great thoroughness, until we felt that we had eaten roast beef and tinned pineapple in all the best houses in the city. We met the Director of the Swedish Iron Ore Company, the City and District Judges, the Doctors, the Parson, the Veterinary Surgeon, the Police Chief, and the higher officials of the Railway—all friendly and well-meaning people. And yet it seemed that these men and women were not the city. They were all, more or less, people in transit. Soon they would be on their ways again. They had come from the Outside and their dream was to move south once more.

Of course, they admitted, Narvik was a beautiful place to live in, especially at midsummer. The mountains, the ocean, the ever-changing colours were breath-taking. But, after all, there was a saying up here that summer came only every fourth year, and, as we certainly would learn for ourselves, the winters were dark and burdensome, and the distance from Oslo and the other great cities was altogether too great. Here there was no theatre, no art gallery, no symphony concerts, not even a lively café where interesting people gathered.

We asked about the other side of town life, the people who had built it and who made their homes here.

The workers on the railway and at the Iron Company constituted the mainstay of the town. They were all organized and the Labour Union possessed the only great hall in town. There the City Council held its meetings and travelling stock companies staged their plays. There was perhaps some truth in the statement that the city spirit was dominated from the Labour Union Centre. The town had been governed by Labour from its very beginning. Young and vigorous as it was, it had not much in the way of tradition, but it did have a history of its own.

In the nineties a British company had begun to buy up the land with a view to exploiting the Swedish iron-ore deposits. The plan was to build a railway through the mountains, across the narrowest part of Norway, to the half-moon-shaped bay below Fagernes Mountain, where a peninsula extends into the Ofotfjord. Streets were laid out for a city to be called Victoria Harbour.

A great construction gang, supplemented by peasant boys and fishermen, worked for months in the mountains. Then the company went bankrupt. When, one Friday, the wages stopped, the job was deserted, and tools and equipment were left scattered about. The project was abandoned. The right of way reverted to the elements. The doors of the empty barracks swung on screaming hinges.

Then the Norwegian Government took it over and completed the railway from the Swedish border down to the harbour. The city was built and named Narvik after the lonely homestead and small trading post that lay inside the tip of the half moon.

A railway station was built on the other side of the peninsula for passenger traffic, but the heavy ore trains moved slowly through the centre of the town, cutting it in two.

Oscarsborg, the business district, lay on the side towards the mountain. Along the low, forested ridge on the outside of the peninsula, protected from the cold winds of the open fjord, lay Frydenlund, the best residential section. The Parkway was the finest street in Frydenlund, and on it were the great one-family houses of the Company officers and engineers.

Most houses in the town, however, were two-family dwellings built by the workers themselves. The owners lived on the second floors and rented the best rooms until the mortgages were reduced. All the houses had small, fenced "rose gardens" in which the owners took great pride. In northern Norway all garden flowers are called roses because of their size and rarity. The wild flowers are usually small, with strong fragrance and vivid colouring.

In the Frydenlund park stood the town's great stone church. It had been designed by a famous architect, who had planned it to be viewed from the south, so that the tower with its slender spire stood between the heavy dome of Fagernes Mountain and the leaning horn of Rombakstötta.

The Market Place was at Oscarsborg, a large open quadrangle faced by the old Post Office and Telegraph Building, with enclosed market stalls built into the hill beneath it. When we arrived, the Market Place was still under construction. The town's wealthy but unpopular banker had donated a fountain which was to be inscribed with a copper plate. The city fathers accepted the fountain but declined the copper plate.

The bridge led directly from the Market Place. Its beautiful bronze lamp-posts were not held in too high favour by the townspeople. They had been bought secondhand from a small town in the South which had installed larger ones.

The railway tracks ran under the bridge, extending in a fanwise net towards the harbour. Between the tracks lay the ore heaps in huge, prim cones. From the bridge the great steamers in the harbour were barely visible, but the roaring rumble of the ore streaming into the hulls could be heard day and night.

Across the harbour was a wooded ridge above which a mountain towered. The top of the mountain resembled the profile of a woman. It was called the Sleeping Queen. A veil of ice and snow always lay over the forehead and eyes, but the nose, a bit on the long side, remained snow-bare until late August.

Above the Market Place was the City Hall. It had originally been a hotel with gay life and illegal brandy. It retained its tower at the corner and the huge, draughty windows on the first floor. Here the Municipal

Court had been installed, where the town drunks were sentenced. On the second floor was the Mayor's office, and in the attic the Taxation Division wrestled with the problem of the city's ever-rising taxes.

Such was the city, simple and surveyable. One never ran the risk of getting lost in it. At a dinner party on the Parkway we were told that the citizens were just as simple. I asked whether this hard land did not make its imprint upon the people.

"Yes, the girls are wild during the summer," the regimental lieutenant said encouragingly. "They become playful from the long Midnight Sun."

"Oh, I rather think it comes from eating too much fish," his blonde wife, my dinner partner, interrupted with a laugh. "The farther north they live, the more fish they eat."

"And where do you come from?" I asked.

She laughed again and said she was born in Hammerfest not far from North Cape. I was more cautious the rest of the evening.

It was self-evident that Narvik was a democratic town without any truly wealthy people. The merchants went bankrupt each time there was a depression and started all over again. The higher officials, the doctors, the dentists, and the lawyers used their money to heat their large homes during the winters, or they put it aside with the idea of moving south again.

The city itself was clean and orderly. Each evening, after supper, which was taken at eight o'clock, we went for a walk, usually on Street 1. The name of the main street was King's Street, when one wanted to be correct, but its common name was just Street 1. When the city was built the streets were given numbers before they were named, and the numbers stuck.

On calm and clear evenings there were always people walking up and down Street 1, people with children, walking sticks, and dignity, or only with dignity. The walking tempo was slow and sedate; no one was rushed for time, no one was going anywhere in particular, and the street lasted longer at a slower pace. And one always greeted with the hat. God, how one greeted with the hat! Not only to ladies or elderly gentlemen, but to everyone. All the men agreed that this hat-greeting procedure was a silly custom that should be abolished, yet no one had the courage to flout tradition.

Psychologically, this irrational slavery to traditional "dignity" may have covered a certain shy reticence. There was, for instance, the young red-haired girl in the tobacco store on the corner of the Market Place. For ten years I was to buy tobacco and razor blades over her counter. We exchanged objective remarks on the state of the weather, the quality of tobacco, and the efficacy of throat tablets. For herself, she preferred the fresh air of Street 1, and thus became one of the many reasons that I wore out my hats in quick succession. Yet, through all those years and hats, she never honoured me with more than a barely visible puckering of the lips in what might have been construed as a vague smile of condescension. At first I thought she was supercilious, yet I must be a good customer since my purchases of tobacco were on the upward trend. Then I became fearful lest she thought I was teasing her, though her change was as correct as her advice on tobacco. As the years went by, her correct smile remained the same enigma of friendly condescension. Finally, I realized that it was in this manner that decent people with respect greeted one another in a decent town.

These evening promenades were not completely devoid of purpose. Every Friday night the express steamer, *Nord Norge*, the city's own boat, departed for the South. The Ofoten Steamship Line had given painful birth to a little fleet of ships plying the broad fjord from Lofoten to Narvik. *Nord Norge* was the pride and prize of this community effort. She sailed the express route to Trondheim and return. Except for the Iron Ore Railway into Sweden, Narvik, like all towns in northern Norway, depended upon sea communications. Great and small steamship companies fought for the best places of call. Most of these companies had subsidies, which gave the Government control over the communications. The system worked for equity in bringing the mail in a short time into the most distant places in the isolated fjords.

The fact that the regular express steamers never called at Narvik remained always an open wound. The daily express communications from Bergen or Trondheim bypassed Narvik in order to save some expensive seven or eight hours from the running time across the Ofotfjord via North Cape to Kirkenes, near the border of Finland. Narvik, with its ten thousand people, was, after all, only two hundred souls behind Tromsö, its neighbour city in the North. But the citizens of Narvik took consolation from *Nord Norge*, their own steamer.

Town officials and business men sailed away and returned on *Nord Norge*. The Town Singers in white caps and blue jackets often enlivened the scene. Sea gulls screamed above the ships in the harbour, and there was the smell of seaweed and tar. Perhaps the band was on hand to play a Sousa march.

The pier was always a focal point of activity, and the stroll down Street 1 often led to it. "The whole town stood on the dock or in open windows waving good-bye," a poet of the local press had written in one of his spring poems.

There were three newspapers in the city. Their schedule of publication was so arranged that the editors might attack one another in turn. On only one point was there complete agreement: that Narvik was the harbour of the world. Unsung and hidden away, it lay like an outpost toward the silent arctic in the service of mankind. Rocked on the swells of the warm gulf stream, the ships kept coming to load the heavy ore, the basic metal for the ploughshare that was destined to turn the furrow of civilization. Each of the newspapers had its own house poet. One of them specialized on early spring.

It is somewhat of an exaggeration to speak of spring in northern Norway. Winter clothing was needed the whole of June. But one morning summer definitely arrived. A calm and comfortable warmth filled the air. A shining transparence spread itself over the heavens, making a thousand different colours come to life in the mountains, the fields, and out on the ocean, until sea and horizon merged in a far-distant embrace. This was the prelude to one long continuous summer day that would last without sundown until the first chill of autumn in mid-August. The Nordic summer had come at last, with sun, day and night; and Nature, in man and beast, drank of its light and warmth. It seemed that life received this re-creating miracle with all its senses open, before the long winter night would again close in.

This was our first summer in northern Norway and we had to take it all in. We had to climb the mountains, wade in ice and snow, hike over the lonely plains with deep and silent lakes, dark with the mysteries of winter and spring. And we had to take a boat trip to the islands in the fjord.

There were three boats. We were to row for an hour or so from the boat harbour north of the town to Øyjord, a small peninsula on the other side of Rombaksfjord, where there were some low, wooded cliffs, ideal for picnicking.

Mr. and Mrs. Einar Mosling were the host and hostess. He was the proprietor of the bookshop and represented the only old family in town. Hardly more than a generation ago there was only the one lonely farm in Narvik, on the inside of the half-moon-shaped harbour. On this fertile, flat soil there had been a habitation since time immemorial. Two generations ago a trading post had appeared where people from inner Ofoten brought their wares and bought their necessities. The Moslings were known as old and fair tradespeople even at that early date. Then the town came. The good soil was turned into streets with new houses, shops multiplied, and business dealings became more complex. The last generation retained nothing more than the name and a bookshop. The bookshop was the only one in the town and the business of being a bookseller might have been quite good. Mr. Mosling, however, was all things besides, and

Dutch Vice-Consul too. Since we were newcomers and from the Colonel's house, we were placed in the host's boat.

The second boat was that of Dr. Paus, who came from the seacoast north of Bergen, where people have sharp gutturals and sharp elbows. Mrs. Paus had been something of a beauty but was regularly having a child. With the doctor and his large family were Engineer and Mrs. Toft. He was Administrative Counsellor of the Railway and might become District Superintendent when the incumbent got a stroke. Mrs. Toft was president of the local Red Cross.

In the third boat sat Lawyer Nils K. Nilsen, whom I had visited on an earlier occasion. He had minced no words in warning me that it would not be wise to try to start a lawyer's practice in Narvik, if one had not been born in the high North. Today he wore a sports suit complete with leggings, and a curved pipe. His facial expression indicated that he did not think our presence quite necessary for a successful picnic.

Our boats slid smoothly across the mirror-like sea between the islands. The oars squeaked a little until we poured water on them. The contours of the mountains were sharply silhouetted against the bright blue sky. The sun was still fairly high, but had begun to take on the glowing reddish-purple hue.

The odour of seaweed mixed with the smell of tar from the boat. Sea gulls sailed through the air, now and then diving to catch a fish or a floating piece of green growth. Their hoarse screams filled out the tonal quality of the sea symphony. The picture of the rugged mountains in the strangely glowing light is not complete without this smell of sea and shore, this sound of bird and ocean, the regularly beating breath of the sea as it licks the wet stones on the shore. In the crystal clear water sea plants rose and fell in slow rhythm. We rowed through narrow inlets between naked stone islands. Farther in, we met heather and wild flowers and crooked pine trees that storm and sea had given fantastic shapes.

At Øyjord we beached the boats and built a fire. The children played with shells and sea-worn stones. Others played games. The men were put to work. The Moslings said that there was enough food, so that only two fishermen would be needed to get the catch for supper. Salt-water fishing is not regarded as either an art or a sport, so Engineer Toft took me, as the newcomer, along with him in the smallest skiff.

It was fairly obvious that he had been taking my measure. He said he understood that I had taken an active part in student politics at the University, and on the Red left wing at that. I saw no reason to deny it.

In his young days he had been a radical himself, he confided, a Red firebrand. But life had taught him a few lessons.

B

I am afraid my smile was a bit cynical. Perhaps he realized that his opening had been a little on the arrogant side.

"Let me put it this way," he said. "One doesn't become wiser as time passes on. Rather, things seem to become more complex and difficult."

"We who are young don't think that life is easy, either," I answered, "but we do think that improvement is possible."

"Granted. But it is hopeless to try to impress a new and alien pattern upon society. Men must first be reformed themselves."

"But the majority of people are more or less what their environment makes them. If we could create more secure and fair social conditions, perhaps even people might be improved in quality."

"And so you want to abolish capitalism and militarism in order to build a community of fraternity and eternal peace?"

I was inclined to let it stand at that. "Something in that direction, yes." The discussion was too general to be of interest.

We continued to fish in silence.

When we returned to the party on shore, the ladies held the preposterous view that it would take too long to fry our catch. Sandwiches, cakes, and coffee must suffice, they said. Of course, the ladies won.

The sun had just barely touched the mountain peaks and was ascending again. The light was soft, and in the quiet we could hear the sea and the gulls. An intoxicating tension filled the air. How was it going to be possible to sleep through these sunlit nights?

During the evening Mr. Nilsen, the lawyer, made me the object of his special attention. He realized that I had made up my mind to open a law office and, even though there would be few spoils to share, he wanted to bid me welcome as a colleague.

He asked me how I intended to begin.

Well, I would hang out my board and see what happened. Perhaps I would even move about a bit among the people until they showed an inclination to come to me. I was even contemplating an office day once a week in Ballangen, the small mining town on the south side of the fjord. It might be easier to become known in a place even smaller than Narvik.

Most certainly a good idea, but it would take patience.

I had to admit that patience was not one of my strong points, but said that I at least intended to try.

Mr. Nilsen was silent for a while, seemingly lost in contemplation of the awe-inspiring scene. Then he made a suggestion, as though he had just thought of it.

Since I was going to stay here anyway, perhaps I would like to start as a junior partner in his office. There would be a monthly salary, and it would rise as I became more experienced.

The proposal caught me somewhat off guard. But this was marvellous! It would mean security, and no starting expense. I could begin working at once, with nothing to worry about. I thanked him, and said I would think it over.

On the way home the reddish tone above the mountains had again given way to a white light. Another working day was at hand. And certainly this was a land to work in. Perhaps, all things considered, the thrill of the struggle would be worth more than security. And that, after all, had been our real reason for coming up here.

II

Law and Order

ACCEPTING a junior partnership with a fixed salary certainly seemed to be the most sensible thing to do, but it did not appeal to us. We went for many long walks discussing our poor chances of establishing an independent law practice in Narvik, and from these walks we at least learned something of the surrounding country. The road into the Beidsfjord was the only one that led to any particular destination. A little village lay at the foot of the fjord.

Ellen said that we must become acquainted with the natives. The people of the Parkway did not look as though they had a great need for lawyers, and, if any of them wanted a divorce, it was unlikely that they would come to me.

Halfway into the fjord I recalled that there was at least one native we might try to meet when we had come this far. It was from somewhere around here that one could get a view of the troll on the opposite side of the narrow fjord. It was a tall moss-covered stone close to the shore line, and would have the exact likeness of a giant with a hanging jaw, if one got hold of him from the right angle. It was one of the tourist attractions. We walked back and forth at the turn of the road from where one should look. There was nothing to see. We did not want to be taken for tourists and so did not inquire from people who passed by. At length we did shout across the narrow fjord to an old fisherman who could have no interest in us anyhow. He did not answer but merely scrutinized us from the shore. We shouted again. Then we discovered that it was unnecessary. It was the Beidsfjord Troll himself.

We agreed that it would be wise to make a humble beginning. At a party a few days before, the old District Judge had lamented the fact

that he must hold court in many different places during the summer
and that he was without a secretary. Members of his office staff had shown
no inclination to sacrifice their holidays even though justice was threatened.
Could I come to the rescue? The position carried no salary, but I might
learn a few things. Ellen agreed that this was probably the proper start, and
that perhaps my association with the District Court would tend to offset
my youthful appearance in the minds of the people in connection with
matters of law and order.

Thus it happened that I became a member of the Court party which
for fourteen days was out to establish justice throughout the district. I
carried the Judge's wooden box, which contained the law books and the
public records. I was to be of general usefulness to the Judge and to act
as Court Reporter, and I was also expected to supply a certain amount of
entertainment.

It was just as well, I thought, that my friends in Oslo could not hear
me. It was not easy to disregard either tradition or the wooden box of
court records, but I felt that the latter was really heavier than need be.
It was a massive box, heavy even without the books. There was a new
set of lighter leather bags available, imprinted with the Royal Seal, but
the father of the District Judge had been District Judge before him, and
he had used the wooden box to house the statutes and the ink bottles,
so there was no help for it.

Most of the journeys were made in the small, overworked steamboats
which zigzagged hither and thither throughout the fjords. A case of
oleomargarine would be left on the dock on the south side of the fjord,
a barrel of syrup at the grocery store on the north side, plus mail bags
with the Royal Lion insignia. Farther south a case of tinned fruit might
be unloaded.

Our first port of call was Sjomen, an arm of the fjord that cuts through
the mountain range south of Narvik.

The Court was called to order in the white-painted schoolhouse by the
church. The litigant was a sewing machine company of Oslo. It was
represented by an attorney from Narvik. The defendant was one Hans
Nilsen Frostisen, who was his own lawyer.

He had bought an electric sewing machine on time payments from a
travelling salesman who had been around during the last Lofot fishing
season. Admittedly there was no electricity on his farm, but the agent
had explained that one would have to take into consideration what would
be likely to happen. Before he had paid up his contract the wonder of
electricity would, most certainly, have found its way even to Sör-Sjomen,
the agent had assured him. The most reassuring rumours were abroad,
even down to distant Oslo, that rural electrification would soon cover

even this fjord district. The payments were small, but many. And as to the risk, that was negligible. As the agent had said, he did not risk anything further than that the sewing machine would be taken back and, then, it would not be his anyhow till he had paid for it. And now he had not met his payments. In fact, he had not gone any further than the cash amount given in down payment out in Lofoten, and one of the monthly payments. That had been almost a year ago.

"Now, it is a fact that Hans Nilsen Frostisen did sign a contract with regard to that sewing machine, didn't he?" asked the Judge.

The old farmer admitted signing the contract, but said that he had no more money and could not meet the payments.

But under such circumstances he could not expect to keep the sewing machine?

No, he didn't expect that. In fact, he had boarded it up in the very same box and carried it in his rowboat over to the mail pier to be returned. He would call the postmaster as witness of this fact. But now the sewing machine people would take his homestead, the very farm of Frostisen which had been in his family's possession for two hundred years.

The lawyer for the company referred to the contract. The legal conditions of a sale were established. The company was merely interested in getting its payments. It wanted only a judgment for payment of the contracted obligation. If, later, it asked for security in the form of a mortgage on the farm, such a procedure would not exceed the rights of the firm in question.

"What is your answer to all this, Mr. Nilsen?" the District Judge inquired in a friendly tone.

"They may take the machine, they may put me in jail, but they must not take the homestead," he answered.

"There is no question of prison or homestead. I don't think you get the point, Mr. Nilsen," the Judge broke in. His patience appeared to be wearing thin.

"I know I am an unlearned and simple-minded man, Your Honour, but I do understand that they are out to get the farm."

The old farmer walked across the floor and pointed toward the other side of the narrow fjord. On a light green strip of land some grey old houses were visible between white-stemmed birches which stood like sentinels on watch against the threatening mountain cliffs that overhung the farm on three sides. From between two sombre ridges a glacier protruded like a huge, ice-cold tongue, bluish-green on the sides. It looked as if it were drooling oversized drops into the river, which, in one great fall, crashed straight down into the sea.

"Do I have the permission of the Court to tell the history of that old homestead under the glacier?" he asked.

"If it has anything to do with this lawsuit." The Judge could not find it in his heart to stop the old man.

"That is for the Court to decide. It may be somewhat distant in time. My grandfather was twelve years old when it happened. The avalanche struck and carried all the houses and everything alive with it into the sea. He and his mother were down by the fjord and got safely into a boat. His father, a child in his arms, had almost reached the shore when the avalanche took him. In the barn were a maid and two small girls. They were killed, too. That was the second time it happened, but each time the rest of our family moved back."

"But what has that to do with the present lawsuit?"

"Only this, that I cannot lose the farm. You must not take Frostisen away from us, do you hear?"

The man was calmed down and the Court proceeded.

It is possible that Hans Nilsen Frostisen at the next Lofot fishing season wasted all his cash on a silver brooch and dress material for his wife, but the grey old homestead is still there, and his family will in all likelihood stay there till the avalanche strikes again.

The next case concerned the theft of a windbreaker with leather lapels. It had not been much of a garment at best, but, as the injured party said, a man must be able to hang his coat in his own forests without running the risk of being robbed. The defendant was now employed in the woods on the other side of the mountain and had tramped the whole night in order to be in court in time to hear his sentence. He agreed in principle but insisted that he was without guilt. In the first place, he had found the jacket on the ground, and, secondly, the sleeves had been too long. He had not intended to keep it and had merely forgotten to return it before the sheriff had arrived.

The defence lawyer held that it did not appear that public security in Sjomen was seriously endangered. The defendant received a light sentence, and the owner of the jacket the suggestion that it would be safer in his own closet, and that, besides, it might fit the next man who found it.

Most of the cases seemed to be more largely concerned with principle than with any great loss of property. As we sat in the schoolroom with flies humming at the windows, and the solemn District Judge facing the serious audience along the walls from his seat behind the huge, ink-stained table, there seemed to be something inevitable and foreordained in the simple decisions that were dictated into the Court records.

Respect for law and order is old and ingrown in Norway. The unity of the nation and the inviolability of the laws are basic traditions. The sagas of the Norse kings are learned by the children with their ABC's and fire them with an almost excessive sense of national romanticism. The extent of the fascination of the sagas for the children's minds I rediscovered during the Court's travels.

It happened at Liland, on the north side of the fjord. Liland is an open, pleasant sea village with relatively large houses. The County Sheriff lives there, and the King's Highway runs as a main thoroughfare the length of the county. The highway follows the shore line, bending and unbending through the widely scattered farms. Where the side road comes up from the steamship pier one finds a country grocery store, the windows plastered with notices about taxes and military service, county council meetings, and public dances. A little farther up, on the other side of the road, stands the "hotel," the ancestral home of two spinsters who found it too large for their needs and so let rooms to respectable tourists. Next to it is the schoolhouse.

The local steamer had arrived ahead of schedule. There had been no cases of oleomargarine to be left at the pier on the south side. No business was scheduled for the afternoon, but we were to hold a brief legal hearing in the evening. The midwife of the valley had accused the postmaster of reading her mail, and he had sued her for libel.

It was the first day of Court of the second week of travel. The Judge was taking his midday nap in the hotel. We had eaten an early dinner and school was still in session. Some of the witnesses were loitering outside the schoolhouse, where the ground was worn from the bare feet of the children, leaving the grass growing only along the fence and the schoolhouse walls. The County Sheriff had found himself a seat on the ground and pondered with closed eyes the welfare of the community. He had left his cap at home and hence was not in uniform, but a heavy leather bag revealed the fact that he was out on legal business.

The sunshine was warm and enjoyable as I lay down in the grass next to a young fellow from the village store, who had been called as a witness. We were too lazy to be formal and simply enjoyed the warm rays of the sun against the schoolhouse wall. Through the open windows we could hear the friendly, slightly droning voice of the teacher and the quick answers from the pupils. He made them repeat the old dictum of the saga: "On Law the Land must be built." It seemed to be the history lesson for the day, or perhaps it was nothing more than an additional attraction, since it happened to be the day when the Court was in session in the village. Whatever it was, we heard about the Constitution and the unity of the nation.

"Ten legal codes existed in Norway before it became unified into one nation," the teacher proclaimed, perhaps more for the benefit of his

public out-of-doors than for the edification of the pupils, who seemed
not too impressed. We heard the scraping of a knife into a desk, and the
protesting voice of a girl who had been taken by the hair and was calling
for law and protection.

"Who gathered Norway into one realm?" The teacher found the
time appropriate to call forth a little active knowledge.

"Harald the Fairhaired, in the Battle of Hafrsfjord," the children
shouted in happy unison. The problem seemed to be too simple and
evidently did not warrant the disturbance of the midday restfulness of
the village. The floor was given to a young girl, probably one in the first
row accustomed to answer whenever there was to be a special demonstration of wisdom.

The clear, girlish voice came through the open window, breaking the
dull sleepiness of the summer day. At first there was a certain stiff formality
as the utterances echoed the printed words of the textbook. The saga
was about King Harald who had given an oath that he would let his
hair and beard grow until Norway had become united into one Kingdom. He sailed down the coast and engaged the fleet of the combined
lords and local kings in the Hafrsfjord, right outside the site of the present
city of Stavanger.

"What was the date of that battle, Ingeborg?" the teacher asked.

"In the year 872 Norway was united," answered Ingeborg, changing
the subject, "and Queen Gyda got permission to cut the King's hair,
and since that time the country has remained one realm."

"You are a very clever girl, Ingeborg. Now, perhaps, you can tell us
something about how Norway became christianized?"

Again she repeated sentences from the history text, but soon found
that method too slow, and continued her story in a lively and self-
assured voice. She told how several of the kings had sailed abroad on all
kinds of martial business and how they learned about Christianity and
wanted to try it out at home.

Among them was Olav Trygvason, who had lived in exile with his
mother since he was a little boy and had become a Christian but remained
at the same time a great warrior. When he returned home he built
churches and made people believe in God and put hot dishes on the
stomachs of those who would not.

"I think you can skip that, Ingeborg," the teacher interrupted. "Perhaps
we cannot take the saga quite literally."

Ingeborg had some difficulty in letting go of Olav Trygvason, who
admittedly had not met with too much success in this line of business. To
make up for it, however, he had many other virtues, and really did not have
the time to christianize the country, since he had to be with his warriors.

"But Christianity, Ingeborg."

"Oh, yes. Olav Trygvason was killed in the battle of Svolder in the year 1000, when the enemy trapped him. Afterwards Norway had another king named Olav and he tried to christianize the country. But the land-owners murdered him in battle at Stiklestad in the year 1030. Later on they were sorry and built a church on the spot where he fell. After he died he did miracles and they called him St. Olav and then all the people of Norway put their faith in God."

Ingeborg was out of breath but managed to arrive at a happy ending before the teacher's wife, from her kitchen on the second floor, rang the bell, dismissing school for the day. The teacher was in no hurry to-day, however, as the Court was evidently not yet ready to take over the schoolhouse. He took advantage of the opportunity to emphasize the relationship between Authority and God—His Law in Heaven and the King's Law in Norway—and said that we all would be better off if we obeyed them both. The children streamed out into the sunshine. We heard Ingeborg's voice all over the playground. This was her day. Her small, stiff braids stuck straight out in the air from sheer excitement.

"As to Authorities, the good Lord sometimes makes use of strange specimens," the grocery clerk remarked.

I thought he had been napping in the grass next to me, but even he had evidently been kept awake by Ingeborg with the braids and the hero-kings.

"Out in Svolvær we once had a mad police captain who arrested people for drinking from bottles," he said. "If they drank from glasses it was all right, but poor devils who drank from bottles were locked up. That was when the new laws came to Lofoten regulating the fisheries, so there was ample reason to arrest people anyhow, but that bloodhound of a police captain was too much of a good thing. At length the people took their revenge. When the fishing went bad and they all went around in Svolvær sucking their thumbs and cursing, they threw codfish heads against his windows."

"What good did that do?" I asked. "He was not to blame for the poor fishing."

"Well, there is no Authority except by the Will of God," the boy answered, spitting far into the grass. Suddenly he relented. "It wasn't nice, was it? But it didn't happen again. Fishing was good the next year."

"And I thought you people had such deep respect for the law," I said. "I had planned to practise law in Narvik myself when this District Court is over."

"Oh, we keep within the law most of the time, but we don't like being bossed around as we were in olden days." He gave me a telling smile. "But we do want justice and order. When I find time, I may have a little lawsuit myself. My neighbour has a queer notion about his boundary line. Some people must be lawyers, I suppose," he added good-naturedly.

The travelling District Court was not without its charm. Here in northern Norway, where distances are great and hotel accommodation not always too good, these legal journeys had created their own forms, blending into the social life as part of a living tradition.

The Court sessions were held in city halls, in schoolrooms, or in Labour Union halls. Members of the Court lived in the nearest hotel, such as it was, or on farms accustomed to receiving travellers. The District Judge had the same room on each occasion and the defence lawyers and the secretary theirs, as a rule sharing it with the youngest lawyer.

At dinner the meat platter went first to the Judge, who sat at the head of the table beneath the picture of King Haakon in its gilded and fly-specked frame. The party passed through the doors in order of age, the eldest first. Titles were always used before names except in the case of the District Judge himself, who remained nameless and was referred to only in the third person, even when addressed directly.

The conversation also had its own form. The District Judge was old and insisted upon his dignity. The stories kept within a certain moral standard, although the limit was somewhat flexible. The supply was not impressive.

As a new member of the party I was looked upon as a kind of fresh breath from Oslo and the University. Of course, the Judge said, things down there were not what they had been in his young days. Quite the contrary, from what he had heard. In those days there was dignity in the student life. The young student swung his glass or his girl with cultured restraint and fought for ideals under a lofty heaven. Ideals were pure and the fight was noble.

I admitted that our modern student life was more earthy. The competition was severe. Positions did not stand waiting for us, and our ideals were turned more towards practical life.

"Politics, I suppose you mean," the Judge said, somewhat testily.

"Yes, politics particularly. Most of us were radicals—socialists, bolshevists, anticlerics, and prohibitionists." I thought it opportune to nail to the mast all the pirate colours I could hit upon.

"Yes, yes," he said, rather wearily, I thought, "but what of the student life itself?"

"Well, we lived in cheap rooming houses and studied expensive textbooks. We went to bed late and tried to get up early in order to secure a reading desk in the University study rooms. We heard lectures from professors who were not occupied with other scientific enterprises. We

sat in student cafés in the University basement, where the coffee came
from the city waterworks and the Danish pastry from Osterhaugsgaten's
Lumberyards."

"What do you mean?"

"Oh, it's only a standard joke. The coffee was thin and the cakes dry
as sawdust, but cheap."

"But you had no festivals and discussions?"

"Of course. An endless variety of clubs and forums where we took up
all kinds of questions, some old and dignified but mostly new and offensive.
We debated social and political issues, religion, sex, and psychology."

"But is there nothing left of the old student humour which characterized
our group and made us go out to meet life with a smile when we were
young? Didn't you make fun of your professors?"

"Certainly, but the professors were not too original or queer any more,
at least not the young ones with whom we worked. They cut their hair
and pressed their trousers. But even so we did our best. Off and on we
staged a University show with a masculine ballet and student satire."

"You did? And you made satirical attacks on the educational arrangements, just as we used to? In what way?"

I racked my brains to recall some of those stupid student reviews.
They were no longer regarded as outstanding events in the hard and
examination-ridden student life of modern Oslo. Our days had been
filled with heated discussions of the new and influential ideas. The old-
fashioned student witticisms were like stale beer. The students no longer
felt themselves to be the cream of a privileged class. We started from the
ground. We were about to build something new and we did not know
exactly what to do with the old. Perhaps we did not even see clearly what
we wanted to build. We did realize, however, that we were destined to
struggle our way through a world of appalling difficulties. Our wit had
a bitter touch. We smiled, but our smiles at times may have been a little
cynical. It was not that we felt superior in comparison with our fathers'
simple-minded humour; we just felt different. We, too, were out to
conquer the world. Perhaps we were not such happy warriors, but the
world had become a heavier load to carry.

It was impossible to get the feel of this change across to the old official.
He would not understand, and would probably only come to believe
that we were even more insane and lost than he had pictured us.

Could I recall any of those innocent student witticisms?

In despair I glanced at the thick volumes in the wooden box, those
bone-dry text-books on Law. There was the *Mortgage Law* by Professor
Hagerup. Hadn't there been something about old, boring Hagerup? Not
very amusing, to be sure, but quite innocent.

"At a law school banquet we put on a sketch from the Roman Law: the slave Crassus indicted for manslaughter."

"Good! That's what I mean."

"But he refused to confess. He was threatened with snakes and burning oil. Still he refused. At length a new instrument of torture was carried in and placed on a red velvet pillow. The slave Crassus shivered till his teeth chattered. The procession marched forward until it came before the bar. The Judge commanded the defendant to scrutinize the object on the pillow. It was a book. The slave Crassus screamed a confession. It was Hagerup's volume on Mortgage Law."

"Excellent! And they say that you modern students lack humour. I begin to regain my faith in our youth. But it is unfortunate that the youth of to-day had so little of optimism and conviction. In my time our idealism came from healthier and stronger sources. We believed in the goodness of mankind and the victory of the human spirit. We never got lost in the mire of petty politics. We moved among the stars in an evolutionary heaven."

And there you are still hanging, I thought to myself, even though the earth in the meantime has evolved through one long war and is already approaching the next.

But I held my tongue. It was an unspoken rule that the Judge should have the last word. While I had no desire to seek popularity with the authorities I did wish to be tolerated in the first-class smoking room of A Deck.

When we arrived back in Narvik, having created justice throughout the District for a long time to come, I went to the sign painter on Street 3 and ordered a great white board with name and title. Then Ellen and I went on a tour of inspection to find suitable offices. We found them on the top floor of the brick building in the centre of the town. There were, of course, other brick buildings in Narvik, but Danielsen's brick building was the largest. It was only three stories high, but its red brick and green window frames dominated the scene. In the building there were both a bank and a clothing shop, the latter the largest in town, belonging to Mr. Danielsen himself. On the second floor the town's best doctors had their surgeries.

Mr. Danielsen was one of the town's more colourful characters and usually stood in the doorway of his establishment, immaculate, elegant, and affable, to greet and be greeted by all who passed. To be a tenant of Mr. Danielsen was not without a certain prestige, a prestige which had been fostered by the proprietor himself until it had finally come to be accepted by the townspeople with benevolent tolerance. For the prestige, no extra charge was made in the rent.

III

We Practise Law

FROM our new office windows we enjoyed a glorious view of the harbour and the rugged mountains to the south of the town. The first days we only sat from 9.30 a.m. until 2.30 p.m. and from 4.30 p.m. until 7 p.m., except Saturday afternoon, as announced on the board. We wondered whether everyone in town was going to pay as little attention to it as the Sleeping Queen, who lay in solemn dignity across the harbour.

Ellen sat in the reception room at the reconditioned typewriter. The furnishings of the lawyer's office itself looked a little too new and unused by contrast.

Much of the time I stood in the open door chatting with the typist, but at the same time giving an impression of brisk activity. Ellen took letters, mostly to our friends in Oslo. They certainly were going to be astonished at this sudden friendliness at midsummer. But in this way we managed to see other papers around us than the inescapable bills for office equipment. We inserted announcements in all three of the town's papers, and the editors printed short news notes about the new law office opened by a friendly young man from Oslo.

Then things began to happen. Clients arrived in numbers beyond all expectations. People came all the time—or almost every day: towns-people and people from the district, for the most part older people.

Cases came in at a great rate, mostly very old cases. An article for young lawyers that I had read had been correct in saying that no great amount of success is needed before a special type of client will flock to a new law office. More papers were in evidence, fat files of completely impossible things, cases which all lawyers for miles around had lost before all the courts that would permit them a hearing. At length I began to inquire whether other lawyers had had the cases before.

"Well, they are all of the same wool."

And here sits a lamb, I mused.

It was imperative, however, not to lose patience, whether it was the woman who fancied people were spitting after her in the street, or the man who had not received any inheritance in spite of the fact that he had defrayed the costs of putting the inheritance uncle in the grave with special handles on the coffin and a heavy tombstone to top it all off. The estate didn't balance, the court had said; there was no inheritance.

But wasn't it a bloody shame to have the deceased parade around, deeply beloved as an inheritance uncle for fifty years, and then, when he finally did pass away—no inheritance?

The problem was to get such people out of the office. I did not see my way clear to charge them for this service, although many times the temptation was strong to do so.

What we needed were some real cases, with all justice on the side of our client, all injustice and all the money, or at least almost all, on the other side, and involving problems not impossible of solution. A widow of Sarepta fighting for her urn, perhaps, or orphaned sons struggling for their ancestral farm even if it was located in Ballangen. Alas, such cases were not plentiful. The world admittedly was full of injustice, but wherever the victims did go to wring their hands during that excellent summer of 1930, they did not find their way to the third floor of Danielsen's brick building.

Patience, of course, would win, but it might not be unwise to go to the mountain, since it was by now an established fact that the mountain was not coming to Mohammed. I, therefore, put into effect my plan to keep office hours every Saturday in Ballangen. The express steamer went out from Narvik on Friday nights, bringing me to Ballangen in an hour and a half. But it took most of Sunday to get back to town. After crossing the fjord as many times as was theoretically and practically possible, unloading a Laplander here and a package there, I usually managed to get home for a late Sunday dinner.

For the better part of a year I kept Saturday office in the back room of Widow Carlsen's hotel in Ballangen. The arrangement did not yield much wealth nor great experience but it was not without some benefits. I mixed with the people and at length I felt that I *knew* Ballangen. According to the census, Ballangen consisted of three thousand souls, but that figure included the whole country to the south of the fjord. And from out there people could, if need be, travel with greater ease to a lawyer in Narvik. The village proper, situated at the foot of the fjord, is nothing but a cluster of homes with a few hundred sleepy but good souls. But three miles up in the valley lies Bjökråsen where there are sulphur mines and life and almost a thousand inhabitants. In addition, there was Milk Valley, occupied by Laplanders with small farms and big families.

Almost all the people in the country districts of northern Norway have farms, at least on the side. The miners have their farms, and even the majority of the fishermen cannot do without their plots of ground. Right up into naked tree-bare Finmark, agriculture remains, in spite of all, the one sure source of livelihood. The potatoes never fail, and there is always some hay for the cattle, even though the corn needed for feed must be imported.

In Mrs. Carlsen's back room I was introduced to the social and political problems of this valley community. The workers formed the strongest group, even though the two or three other political groups retained a plurality on the County Council. The political situation was in many respects identical with that in many other places throughout the country or with that of the National scene. In Parliament, the small centre party, the Left, sat in power with a National Cabinet. And in Ballangen, Post Carlsen, the Postmaster, was Mayor. Mr. Carlsen was a man of humour and tolerance, by his own statement, a virtue of necessity. There would soon be barely enough Liberals left for a bridge foursome, yet they were the only ones who knew how to run the community.

The Township is a real force in such a small society. If unemployment strikes, the Township provides extra work; it is duty-bound to care for its people. It extends credit in dealings with respect to the Land Bank, the hospital, and even down to the cabinetmaker who makes coffins.

"Communal self-government is a fine idea," Post Carlsen commented, "even though it is slavery to those who sit at the top."

"But why did you accept such a job with no pay and all trouble?"

"Well, my party nominated me, and after all someone must be Mayor. My father lived here before me and my children will perhaps continue to live and work in Ballangen. This is our history and it is fun to have a part in its making. Nothing much happens here in Ballangen, but it is not without interest to have a place in the game. After a while one gets pretty good at playing one's cards."

He explained the working of the game.

The Township played with the Government as its partner. The State was distant and vague, and its cards lay on the table and were played by the Township. The State held the trump cards. Without its authority and resources the play could not continue.

The other players were the Co-operative and the Mining Company.

The Co-operative meant the miners and most of the peasants in the immediate neighbourhood. The private merchants were without financial resources and there was no bank in the community. Anyone could buy at the Co-operative store, but only members participated in the bonus. Because of its well-knit organization the Co-operative had a certain political importance. It did not hold much of a hand, but its cards were played with passion and optimism.

Who was really behind the cards of the fourth player, the Mining Company, was never clearly brought out. At first it had played for large stakes, but later only to keep things going. On solemn occasions statements were issued to the effect that all that mattered was to keep the mines open for the employees, and in that manner it appeared to join the interests of the Co-operative. It was felt in some quarters that another reason for their continued operation was to protect what was left of the original investment.

Björkåsen Mines had originally been a stock company. It had gone bankrupt and had been reconstructed several times. The holders of the mortgages in the company's properties were the real owners, even though it never seemed possible to get to the bottom of those property rights. The Company never paid income taxes, as it never showed a profit, and yet the sulphur went out of the valley in a now thin, now heavy, but never-ending stream. The little engine kept steaming asthmatically up and down from the mines in Björkåsen to the loading piers at Ballangen. Back and forth, puffing and wheezing, always on the verge of capsizing on the sharp curves but never quite succeeding. By sheer force of custom, the lilliputian train seemed always to get through, arriving safely all out of breath at the warehouses next to the pier. There were no accidents save when a cow or sheep, off and on, went through a fence to let itself be run down by the locomotive.

"The peasants evidently train their cattle for this particular purpose," the Mining Director used to complain when we came to his office with our clients' claims.

"Oh, no, we are really afraid that our cattle may get your whole train in the wrong throat and contract stomach infection from sulphur," was the client's common retort.

Compensation for lost cattle was made at fixed prices and usually did not require legal assistance. A lawyer was needed only when the cow was with calf and, therefore, warranted a somewhat higher price. Naturally enough, it usually happened to be a pregnant and slightly absent-minded cow which had the misfortune to be on the wrong side of the fence. It was, therefore, a rather simple matter to figure out the compensation: "One cow, 'Litagod' and practically one calf." The Company usually paid. The Director was a humane man with a keen sense of humour, but he limited himself to *one* calf.

One thrifty little Laplander from Milk Valley vociferously claimed twins, and was deterred from taking the case to court only by the expense involved. His sense of injury and desire for satisfaction were in no way lessened when the Mining Director, in exasperation, finally said, "You had better watch your wife, my dear man. Even she might find a hole in the fence one of these days."

I was to have much to do with Laplanders during the next ten years, so it was fortunate that I had the opportunity, while in Ballangen, of learning something about them. As farmers they are not successful, but in the mines and at hard labour they get along fairly well. They live in the present moment and share with all primitive races a dislike of any long-range planning. They need a driving force since they have lost for all time the natural freedom of their primitive reindeer existence. Tuberculosis has wrought havoc among the Laplanders of northern Norway. Approximately twenty thousand are left, and it is safe to assume that that number will remain fairly constant. Social and medical welfare work have corrected the worst defects. There are no laws of discrimination against the Laplanders and they have not been made the victims of any race prejudice. There is, perhaps, a touch of condescension in dealings with them, which can be bad enough, but this attitude does not apply to the individual Laplander of proven ability in society.

"You can even marry a Lap girl," said Post Carlsen, "if you can find one who is attractive enough."

The reindeer Laplanders are proud of their origin. They call themselves *Samer* and retain their native, original language. They wear their own picturesque clothes, baggy blouses, called *kofte*, made either of leather with the fur on the outside, or of black cloth, gaily decorated with borders of red and green, and hung with tassels. The caps are of odd shapes, some resembling stars, others small, broad skis, with tassels at the points. Each tribe has its own peculiar pattern.

The other Laplanders, who have settled among Norwegians, are called *Bulapper*, and they strive hard to conform to the modern mode of living. They have discarded the customary Laplander dress but keep the *komagers*, a soft leather moccasin without stiff soles or heels. Filled with a special kind of dry grass, they are the warmest footwear known. In the *komagers* the Laplanders glide with the greatest ease across the mountain plains, their bowlegs and crooked knees making them recognizable at great distances. Their knives dangle in their great sheaths, and red tassels swing in the wind. Their round faces with the high cheek bones are brown and baked by sun and storm. A narrow mouth smiles a broad smile in a beardless face. Their teeth are, generally speaking, poor, from improper diet. The Laplanders are small of stature and narrow-skulled. They are a friendly people, mingling a sense of fantasy with limitless curiosity.

For the benefit of the tourist traffic they tend to exaggerate their supposed peculiarities and oddities, their superstitions and magic. In any Laplander camp shown as a tourist attraction there will easily come to be too many reindeer in artistically overdone carvings on knives and utensils. The Laplanders have discovered that tourists want things as fancy as possible. The things they make for their own use are often characterized by a truly artful simplicity.

So far as the mysterious magic is concerned, that is pretty well worn-out by this time. An ancient Lap woman in Milk Valley knew the art. She could *gane*, people said, putting disease and affliction on man and beast. But she never practised except where love affairs were concerned.

I asked an intelligent old Laplander about these things. He was a retired teacher and a very happy person. With a somewhat sad smile he said he was proud of being a Laplander. But he wore neither *kofte* nor *komagers*.

"Why do you people always have to ask about these evil practices?" he asked. "With primitive life there are always certain mystical secrets. I do not know whether there is much in it, but there are many Laplanders who have the power to stop bleeding. The physicians don't believe it, but they do not object to our trying it, and the wound does not bleed any more."

We sat talking in Widow Carlsen's garden. Teacher Sarri wished to talk with me, if I could spare a moment from my office, so we had moved outdoors. I understood that he did not want to be regarded as a new client.

If I were interested in business, there would soon be a case in Milk Valley. A young girl in trouble. The case would not be up for another month or so. And, if the fat son of the grocery owner came around, would I please tell him that I had already been engaged? It was Inga in his neighbour's house. She was barely seventeen.

And of young Inga's sad and short romance I was going to hear again and again until it was all concluded in a prosaic statement between stiff covers with an official stamp, reducing the whole dream about life and love to a monthly payment of fifty shillings.

As time went on my Ballangen files, little by little, received legal material. Deeds were written, tax complaints were made out, and other legal statements were addressed to the authorities and the courts.

When former clients visited Narvik they usually called at my office frequently bringing friends or relatives with them. Things began to take shape. Now it was ordinary people who came, people who did not

especially want to consult a lawyer but who had been forced by circumstances to do so. They were mostly minor cases and few of them went on
to court.

Sometimes cases came to me from even other districts than Ballangen.
One day towards autumn a firm peasant woman entered the office.
She wore her black Sunday dress and had a silk scarf about her head.
It was difficult to get a clear picture of her case, but we took our time.
At intervals, Ellen, who still served as office assistant, would come in
with papers to sign. Instant silence broke our discussion and my wife-
secretary disappeared in a hurry.

I took notes, and at the close of our conversation found it necessary
to make a summary of the whole affair. Her name was Amanda and she
was engaged to the owner of Tykkskog in Kjeldbotn. The engagement
had lasted for twenty years. One Saturday night many years ago Lars
had proposed marriage, and he had made the proposal many times since.
She had lived on the farm all that time. Marriage had not materialized.
Now he was past eighty and sick in bed. The doctor had little hope, and
Amanda did not know whether she should call the parson or the lawyer.
She had come to the lawyer.

"And Lars Tykkskog is still of a sound mind and willing to sign such
a will in the presence of witnesses?" I asked.

"Lars has promised me both the farm and marriage since I was
eighteen."

"But does he remember this now?"

"Oh, yes, he remembers it all right. Now he even talks about the
parson."

"Perhaps he wants to confess his sins?"

"No, he wants us to get married, but now I don't see that it makes
any difference. If we are married, I will receive only half the property,
as I would have to share it with a nephew of Lars who lives in Lofoten.
A legal will would be better for me."

"And Lars wants me to come along?"

"He gave me a cow to get to town. I sold her to the butcher and the
question now is whether you will come with me. We can catch the local
steamer this afternoon, and you can return on the milk boat."

Amanda and I took the steamer to Kleldbotn, which lies at the mouth
of the fjord to the south of the town. It was late when we arrived and
only a few people were on the dock. The agent, observing that she had a
strange gentleman companion, greeted Amanda politely. She acknowledged the greeting, but it was clear that she did not wish to enter into
conversation. We marched silently along the main highway until we
turned left on a trail leading up to the forest-clad ridge.

The midnight sun was gone, but its light touched the mountain peaks, causing the patches of snow to glow with a red-violet reflection. The pine woods were dark and colourless, but there was a delightful aroma of wild berries and heather. Suddenly the forest opened and there, on a slightly sloping plain, lay Tykkskog. The small unpainted house was next to the wooden fence. The barn, a little farther down, had once been red, but that was long ago. The buildings lay as though they had been created simultaneously with the mountains and the woods at the dawn of time.

Amanda had marched in silence like a soldier. She halted suddenly at the opening in the fence and dried her brow.

Wasn't this a beauty spot? She had carried water from the pump at the back of the house every day for twenty years. She had cared for the cattle and baked the bread. The stove filled with heavy smoke when the wind blew against the cliff, but it was a good stove and always gave even heat. Tykkskog was the first place in the valley to see the sun after the winter darkness. It lay so high and free. It was the only place in the world for her.

A bed was made for me in the main living room. We could talk business to-morrow. Her sister and two of the neighbours would be over for breakfast. She had understood that the witnesses must not be relatives.

After coffee and breakfast, and more coffee when the neighbours came, we went in to see Lars. He was still alive. He looked more tired than sick, as though he had decided that his working days were over. We talked about the weather and the valley and the farm. Amanda moved cautiously towards the subject. Lars frowned so hard that wrinkles formed and disappeared in his strong old face. For a moment he seemed to be uncertain which of his promises he was about to be asked to keep. I thought it would be best to speak plainly.

The fact of the matter was that Amanda had called me out from town. She told me that he wished to make his last will about the farm. It was, of course, not absolutely necessary to make any definite will at all. But, if he had arrived at a final decision, I would put into writing whatever he might dictate. Perhaps he wished to speak to me in private first?

Yes, that would probably be best.

I felt that I sat alone with him for an eternity. Flies hummed against the nailed window, while from the open window to the south came the smell of new hay.

It was true, he hadn't treated Amanda right. She had been wife on the farm all these years, but he had never gone through the wedding ceremony. He had promised that many, many times.

But why hadn't he got around to it?

"Well, you see, Mister Lawyer," he said "once I was going to marry the girl on the greatest farm in the valley, but her father objected. She moved into town and I stayed on out here. She was beautiful, small and blonde and full of life."

"Yes, but that must have been ages ago?"

Yes, it had been a long time ago. Since then he had taken life pretty much as it came. And, since Amanda had not had any children anyhow, there hadn't been any great haste. Now it was perhaps too late to bother the parson. But he had certainly brought the farm into fine form; the fields were good and they were free from stones. He was about to leave it now and Amanda should have it all; that was correct enough.

Finally the will was written. In as solemn terms as I could make myself adopt I wrote it on the excellent stamped paper I had brought along. There was both Royal Crown and official stamp on the document. If things had not been too orderly earlier, Lars was at least going to have his last will in decent form and order. The whole thing was somewhat involved, but no doubt remained as to who was going to inherit Tykkskog with all its rights and glories when the signer went to his just reward. He heard the solemn will and winked as the last sentence was read. The witnesses found everything in legal order and signed with great, clear hands. Amanda cried a little and the whole occasion was very formal and proper.

Again we had coffee, and Lars took a nap. The rest of us moved back to the main living room and continued our conversation about the valley. The Lofot fisheries had been pretty poor this season, but the potatoes and the hay looked good. Finally, the witnesses departed.

Some hours still remained of the beautiful day, and I went for a walk. The mountains in northern Norway have a charm of their own. In the southern part of the country there are both plains and higher peaks, but here the forest limit is lower, and Nature gives one everything in one great glimpse; the distant ocean, the crooked pines, the white birches, the bare plateau with its quiet mountain lakes. The land stretches arms out into the ocean and embraces the quiet fjords where fishermen have lived for long generations.

There was something inevitable about the valley down there. It was exactly right that it should lie just where it did.

If I wanted to say good-bye to Amanda, I would have to turn back. It might be a good idea to try to get a little sleep before the milk boat left at 4 a.m.

It was arranged that Amanda should see me to the boat. She had to take care of the milk anyhow. I was up early without being called. Sleep was very light when no dark curtains covered the windows. The wooden bedstead was a trifle short and the cover was heavy. The aroma

of coffee drifted in from the kitchen and I went out and poured myself
a cup from the great copper kettle.

Amanda was in the barn. She sat milking when I came in, looking years
younger in her working dress.

"Are you up already?" she said. "I had planned to bring you coffee
in bed."

I told her I had helped myself and had come out to inspect the barn.

Everything looked clean and orderly. She rose and moved a few
things. In front of an empty stall was a wooden vessel with salt which she
placed on the shelf. She smiled an excuse.

"It is only the farewell meal of Dagros. Lars told me to feed her plenty
of salt the last day, so that she might drink her stomach a little more
round."

"What a pity you have to sell Dagros. Now you will have only three
left," I said.

"Oh, Dagros is getting pretty old, and it is too much work with four.
Personally, I prefer chickens and sheep."

We discussed all kinds of possible improvements as we walked down the
trail. After some debate, she let me help her carry the milk bucket. At
the highway there was one more bucket, so we had one each. Amanda
was not so solemn now. She did not have city clothes on. She joked and
said I might get a job as farm hand, if I failed as a lawyer. There could not
be many such silly old girls in the valley or old bachelors with good
estates and bad consciences. I said I thought she would need a farm hand
under any circumstances. Did she have to carry this milk every morning?
Hardly morning, in fact; even the birds sounded sleepy.

The milk had to go to the dairy in Narvik. But every second week the
neighbour maid carried the milk cans from the crossroad. Then Amanda
had to carry them only that far. She used to leave them in the evening.

"But doesn't it happen that the milk cans sometimes disappear?"

"Why? There is a name plate on each of them."

When we neared the dock, she suddenly grasped my can. I was not to
carry it any longer.

"But that's silly. Give it to me."

"No. There are too many people here. They would think . . ."

"What could they possibly think? After all, when you have lived with
Lars for twenty years, you might—I mean, you can certainly let me help
you carry the milk."

"You don't understand."

"I'm afraid I don't."

"Well, people might think that you are not a real lawyer, and you do
look young, if you will pardon me for saying so."

She kept her burden. We said good-bye with austere formality. The little white boat *Haldis* lay at the dock, her motor idling. Almost on schedule we were on our way.

The milk route was a life necessity to the farmers along the fjord. It was the milk which produced cash for the needed everyday expenses plus the small luxuries, such as coffee, tobacco, and such magazines as limited budgets would permit. The income from milk was the steady source of cash; all other income was more or less sporadic.

The *Haldis* took passengers, and the fares were reasonable, when one took the distances into consideration. She stopped at practically every farm along the fjord. What she lacked in beauty she made up in dependability. Even in wintry storms and high seas she kept her schedule. She was strong and seaworthy, and had an engine that made itself both felt and known. Her explosive coughing shattered the eardrums, while her unbelievable vibration took toll of the nervous system. Sleep was out of the question. To read was impossible, and conversation difficult, if one did not want to exert oneself. The five or six hours in to Narvik was not a pleasure trip.

Soon milk cans filled the deck, and the passengers were driven down into the dim light of the cabin. The place was clean enough but smelled strongly of milk and oil and tobacco.

Despite the difficulties, we could not sit in silence for the entire trip. Most of those aboard were already acquainted. These northern fishermen and farmers have a keen sense of humour, but their sense of propriety dominates their conduct. They seemed a trifle on the cold side and somewhat dull, but then it was not regarded as good form to show too much curiosity. The Laplander who sat on his cheese barrel in the middle of the floor could not restrain his curiosity and finally asked, "Where do you come from?"

I thought I gave him complete and correct information, but he pursued every detail to its furthest point. The shaking of the boat and the noise under the deck made it difficult to talk. We had to shout to each other.

So I was married? Why did I not have any children? Did I have much experience as a lawyer?

Haldis suddenly dived to the side and we had to hang on to our seats, but the Laplander did not lose the thread of the conversation. His teeth clattered so wildly that I was afraid they would break, and they looked new. He was aware of the danger himself and put them into his pocket before continuing with his examination.

Across from me sat an elderly and dignified peasant. He had kept silent the whole time. Now he moved over to my bench and proposed that we go up for a breath of fresh air. We sat on milk cans in the stern of the boat.

He understood that I was new in the fjord and that I came from Oslo. He had lived up here all his life. To-day he was on his way to Narvik to attend the annual meeting of the Co-owners' Dairy.

I expressed an interest in its organization, but hardly realized what I was letting myself in for.

He explained in detail how communications and co-operation had begun to bring confidence and continuity to the hard and insecure life along the coast. Poverty and mutual distrust had been the bane of the peasants for years. At last they had discovered the need for co-operative effort. Small co-owners' dairies were being organized throughout the region and they were bringing profit to the farms and security to the farmers. They were built on the pledges of members to sell all their market milk to the dairy. A stable production meant a stable price level.

The greatest weakness thus far was that there existed no nation-wide organization such as was enjoyed by the great consumer Co-operative.

He stood prophetic before his audience of old milk cans and sleepy me. "We see our way now. It is going to be possible to increase the efficiency and raise the living standards of the peasants, but the Government must use its authority to get them organized. The industrial workers went ahead with their organizing in the face of Government opposition until the trade unions became recognized and finally received the blessing of the State. Our peasants are more individualistic and the development will be some-what different, but it will come. And then the fishermen will come along. When the co-operatives and the trade unions include workers, peasants, and fishermen, this is going to be a fine country. My brother gave up hope and emigrated to America, but I still believe this country can become a good place for the common people.

"My name is Trondsen. I hope I have not bothered you too much, Mr. Lawyer," he wound up. "People out in my valley call me Endless Trondsen."

I assured him that he had never had a more interested audience and that I, too, believed in co-operation and progress. I told him that we city students had some understanding of the struggles and visions of the labour movement and that in them we found a new concept of society and were enthusiastic about it. The problems of the peasants, however, were more distant to us, shrouded somewhat in a cloud of old-fashioned national romanticism. But perhaps milk prices and meat control were just as important as peasant dances.

"At least to us they are," he said. "The struggle for survival these days tends to become so hard that there is little energy left for other things."

We had talked ourselves into Narvik, and Trondsen promised to pay me a visit, which he did some weeks later, with a small legal matter.

At length a certain order and meaning began to characterize the work in the little office. It became alive with human destinies, and a new life opened before us. Had it not been for the necessity of bringing a certain business-like balance to our books, we would have been perfectly happy. The summer went into autumn and the darkness grew on us. It was not easy to keep the belief that we were necessary in this land of the Northern Lights. Law and order seemed to take care of themselves pretty well without our help.

In some fashion we managed to struggle through. We had our own apartment, furnished on the instalment plan. Occasionally we took a few small cases to court, we got a father of sorts to the girl born to Inga in Ballangen, but no really important cases came our way.

The secretary continued to pound the typewriter and often expressed mixed feelings of weariness and optimism at the growing stack of papers. Business must be improving, she thought. I quoted the words of the old farmer when he presented his wife to the King. "Not much to brag about, Your Majesty."

Then I got my great case. It is said that every young man gets one great chance. This was mine. The case itself was rather ridiculous. At least there was no connection between the point at issue and the passions it aroused. The town Banker had injured the honour of a Company Director and vice versa. The latter represented persecuted innocence; that is, he was our client.

Banker Ole Dahl was the town capitalist. He was the owner of all the great buildings in Street 1, at least the most important corner buildings with shops to either side. The economic life of the town had swung up and down, dependent as it was on one single industry. Off and on merchants went bankrupt and their property was sold at auction. The bank took over and the Banker had acquired quite an assortment of buildings. He was a very shrewd business man on behalf of both the bank and himself. Thirty years earlier he had been a carpet-bagger, visiting the temporary barracks which housed the railway gangs. That was at the time when the railway was built from Sweden. There had been a building boom. Much money came and went. Old Dahl's genius was to see that the money always came and never went. He had had no schooling and his knowledge was entirely practical. In many ways he was the mightiest man in town. The one bitter limitation in his life was his sense of inferiority; he knew he was not "fine" enough. He got no invitations from the cultured society. It might have been this feeling which caused his dislike of Director Plöen, who was one of the society leaders.

Certain arguments between them had been aired in the town papers and had got beyond control, so the gentlemen took legal action against each other. The police authorities had rejected their appeals, and they preferred their charges in the civil courts. The Banker retained the most famous lawyer in northern Norway, while the Director had only me, a choice made, no doubt, with certain misgivings.

The case itself was farce comedy. The town's labour population had no love for the Mining Director, but they wished all evil upon the head of the Banker. The business people were filled with secret glee and the Iron Ore Company leaders looked down from their chilly heights upon a most refreshing spectacle. The court room in the City Hall was packed to overflowing for three consecutive days. The City Judge was disqualified in the opening skirmishes and the court proceedings were conducted by a judge from one of the neighbouring towns.

As it happened, the accusations of the Banker, thanks to his acute imaginative malice, were rougher than those of the Director. It was really true that the Banker had exceeded the limits of legal slander while the Director had not. There was no need for extensive legal knowledge or brilliant court-room technique. It was necessary only to aim and fire, and that before an extremely receptive public. We won the case. The Banker was found guilty and received a fine, which, even though it was only for twenty-five shillings, broke his magic power in the town.

We bought a new typewriter and hired an office girl. The law office was successfully established.

IV   *Town Politics*

ALTHOUGH our victory in the "famous" lawsuit did not bring more work into the office, it did result in work for which we began to be paid. The merchants came with documents and bad debts, the Mining Company sent us some cases, and there were occasional calls from the little jail behind the City Hall on behalf of clients who wanted a defence lawyer. As time went on the legal work began to be routine, during the dark winter almost automatic.

Perhaps one is likely to overstress the importance of the dark period in which the sun disappears. The individual day during the three winter months without sun is really not much different from a cold grey day farther south. It is not completely dark, and there is a faint indication of daylight for several hours each day, even though it is necessary to use electric lights. And it is not so cold, after all. Thanks to the Gulf Stream, the coastal temperature rarely drops below 30°. For the most part it is the dull monotony over a seemingly infinite number of days that makes the time seem so heavy.

Perhaps the monotony of the small town is universal, but it becomes a test of character when a colourless sky drops on one's head and dim mountain ranges seem to press in from all sides and the feeling of space is created only by the storms which rage in from the horizonless ocean and whine among the mountains. It is during the dark weeks that one learns to appreciate sturdy homes and pleasant firesides.

Many books are read during the long evenings of the long night. The dark period seems ideally suited to reading. No volumes are too thick, no topics too strange, to be of interest now. All the new Norwegian books were read as a matter of course—Knut Hamsun, Sigrid Undset,

Olav Duun, Arnulf Øverland, and Herman Wildenvey. We also took a keen interest in foreign literature. We discussed Hemingway's simple and direct style and his indirect method of making his characters come alive. We debated the extent to which we might accept the realism of Sinclair Lewis as an accurate description of modern American life. Most of Dickens we had in good translation, and we especially read the *Pickwick Papers*. We had also time for Galsworthy's *Forsyte Saga*. Thornton Wilder's *Bridge of San Luis Rey* provided a topic of discussion for a long time.

Once a week we went to the cinema and saw American films. We found it difficult to reconcile the picture our emigrants had painted for us about a toilsome and not too adventurous life in God's great, new country, with these black and white pictures of sinister gangsters and noble millionaires who married poor but blonde secretaries.

And we played bridge, with some dispute as to the merits of Mr. Culbertson.

Skiing in the mountains was certainly our main attraction especially after work and the chill and the darkness had given in in the beginning of February. We went over the mountains to the Swedish tourist hotels when we got heavy Smörgås and thin beer. All of us had skis.

In spite of these activities, however, we had a surplus of time and a need for other interests. One of our best friends, a lean, good-humoured instructor from Bergen whom we called "Bergenstick," maintained that it was lack of patience with bridge and a stomach that would not tolerate Scotch that drove me into politics. I was to learn that local politics could keep one's hands full.

At first I could not see much connection between the great political visions that had presented themselves during the student days in Oslo and the struggle for justice and power in the town of Narvik. The labour movement in Narvik was old and strong, both as a trade union and as a political force. All the workers of the Iron Ore Company and of the Railroad were organized, and most trade unions had collective membership in the Norwegian Labour Party. The Narvik group comprised more than a thousand members, and the Party, practically speaking, had a plurality on the City Council throughout the history of the town. The Party life consisted in its contact with the leadership in Oslo and discussion of fundamental questions, in Trade Union matters, and, above all, in endless debates and small intrigues concerning local civic problems. Although the squabbles were usually storms in a teacup the waves ran high.

I had been a member of the Labour Party Youth Organization since high school days, and again found it necessary to steer a course between the two common pitfalls, too much theorizing on the one hand and too many social evenings with coffee and *julekake* on the other.

In Narvik there were still repercussions of the split between the Labour Party and the Moscow Communists. As early as 1922 the Norwegian Labour Party had rejected the thesis of the Third Internationale as presented by Moscow. I can still remember the heavy volume printed on cheap newsprint, its unspeakably bad translation bristling with technical and alien phrases. The problems were analysed both as to fundamental theory and from the standpoint of dialectics, and all the dynamic elements had to be taken into consideration. Our discussions resolved themselves into debates for and against the power lines of Leninism. Although we were unwilling to accept the thesis, we were contemptuous of the designation "pink." In any event the Moscow Communists were now in a helpless minority and the sect had steadily shrunk, but there were still small groups here and there of stiff-necked "againsters."

As the Labour Party was in power it was only natural that there should be opposition from the Left on the part of the Narvik Communists who, though not very numerous, were extremely eager and tried to gain some hold through the youth organizations. We had some great political fights.

In the spring of 1931 I was appointed the representative of the Youth Organization on the Governing Board of the Party, the mighty institution that laid out the course, nominated and criticized the Party representatives, and, in short, acted as the moving but perhaps somewhat too talkative force behind our city politics. Membership on the Governing Board totalled more than one hundred, and all members were voluble with personal opinions on all questions. It is quite probable that I did not take the matter very seriously. It was difficult for me to appreciate the importance of minor points in connection with the granting of beer licences to the hotels, or the closing hours of the news kiosks, or whether the firemen should be exempted from the obligation of buying uniforms from money allotted them for that particular purpose.

In any event, I was put to work on *Vergerådet*, the civic committee which handled the intricate problems of broken homes and juvenile delinquency. I consoled myself with the thought that *Vergerådet*, too, had its mission. It was made up of elderly and dignified gentlemen, experienced and bearded, plus the Judge and Parson of the town, the two latter being members according to law.

Our work, as are practically all assignments in city government, was unpaid. The members were chosen by the City Council and were numbered in proportion to the strength of their respective parties: the Labour Party had three, the Conservatives and the Liberals one representative each. Our group had been instructed to fight for the ideals of the Labour movement, but the indifference of parents and the pranks of children did not seem to fall into different political or social categories. Neither in Norway as a whole, nor in Narvik, did we have any juvenile delinquency to speak of, but there were, of course, parents who neglected their children.

. The City Judge and the Parson, as permanent members, gave continuity to the work of *Vergerådet*. They were kindly and humane men and their advice was generally followed. Frequently, after the meetings were over, the Judge, the Parson, and I remained in the Judge's office and talked at length of life and society. The office itself was old and dingy but it afforded a magnificent view of the rugged mountains to the north of the fjord. The Judge was a small and unpretending man with a keen mind, the Parson tall and aristocratic in appearance, a political conservative more tolerant of human beings than of ideas. I was subjected to much bantering about the "terrible" Labour Party in Narvik which was anti-clerical and yet had built the greatest and most beautiful church in northern Norway.

"We wish to be tolerant," I said, not knowing whether to take his words as complimentary or critical.

"I, too," answered the Parson, "and I want to tell you that even though people here, as in so many other places in the country, are poor church-goers, that is no sign that the Church is in danger. The workers here in Narvik still have church weddings and their children are baptized and confirmed. Religious education in the schools is going forward rather than backward. There was a time when things looked pretty bad, and perhaps the Church was partly to blame, but now the danger seems to be over."

"But perhaps the influence of the Church over people and society is not as great as it was in earlier days?"

"True, and yet our spirit is more alive than ever. Here in Narvik, for instance, respect for the needy and the whole problem of social welfare has been handled to an extent that is absolutely marvellous."

"But you cannot maintain that the Church backs these new theories of social security and of society's responsibility to its unfortunates."

"Perhaps we should say that the spirit of brotherly love in human relations is even older than the theories you are talking about."

The Judge usually concluded these discussions with some sound remarks about the parallelogram of forces. The direction of development was a result of many forces. The social struggle within the country had not yet reached its conclusion; but, if one considered Sweden and Denmark as examples, the labour movement in Norway would still progress for some time and finally gain political responsibility and moderation together with political power.

We usually let the Judge have his last word.

Vergerådet was not the only responsibility with which I was entrusted. The following autumn I was asked to start an evening school for labour youth, and in spite of the fact that the teachers received no remuneration, an ample teaching staff was made up of volunteers from the high school and college. There were more Labour Party members among teachers in the high schools than in the grade schools. The main subjects taught were political science, social history, and English. The general results were satisfactory; at any rate, I learned a good deal myself.

It would soon be two years since we had arrived in Narvik, and we had grown rather easily into the life of the town. Glory and reward had not been great, but we were in satisfactory circumstances. We had good friends and good credit. When one knew it from the inside, the town was not so bad after all, and interesting things managed to happen with reasonable regularity.

Thus it also happened that one day we came to own our own home. It was a small yellow house with green window frames out on Framnes Peninsula. A little far out, perhaps, fifteen minutes' walk from the Market Place, but it had an open location on a hillside facing the harbour and was protected from the ocean. One reached it over a winding road which made a little **S** among small pine trees and white-stemmed birches. It was new and complete and modern, and the owner was going south. We took over the mortgage and the name "Kittenshill." From the corner window in the living room we had a magnificent view on two sides: the Sleeping Queen to the south, looking even longer in face from here than from downtown, and Fagernes Mountain to the east, hovering above the city. Straight ahead we had a full view of the harbour, where we counted the ships every morning when we raised the curtains in the sleeping room upstairs.

That summer my parents left for Oslo, but before they left they had seen us settled at "Kittenshill."

My father's successor was a certain Colonel Konrad Sundlo. We knew that he was a reactionary with political ambitions. He was not old-fashioned and high-minded in his conservatism like our ordinary politicians of the Right, but showed extreme sympathy for Fascism. Immediately upon arriving in town he had written articles for the local papers pointing out the Danger from the East. He had once been in Russia and knew some Russian and, therefore, regarded himself as an expert on the Red Peril. He was also anti-British and a Jew baiter. He spoke patronizingly in broad generalities of the working classes and at the same time attacked labour leaders and trade unionists.

It could not be said that he was forceful or dominating in appearance. Short and stocky, he had a flushed, rather formless face. His hobby was to popularize philosophy, and he attempted to redeem his slightly ridiculous personality through speechmaking on strong men and Viking exploits.

In the autumn of the same year I became secretary of the Labour Party in Narvik, and, before I knew it, I was deep in city politics. The problems were not so ridiculous now. The endless debates concerning liquor licences for the hotels continued, and in these discussions the roots of the labour movement history were laid bare. Prohibition was defended not so much by teetotallers from personal conviction, as by the old wheel horses of the labour movement. In earlier days they had seen their meetings broken up and their organization ruined by liquor and noise; they had seen money wasted in heavy drinking, so that union dues could not be paid. As a consequence they had come to hate with a fanatical hatred both the liquor interests and restaurants and bars serving liquor.

The prohibition which followed the first world war had long since been abolished, but the individual township retained the right to determine how the local liquor problem should be handled. The granting of liquor licences to hotels and restaurants was voted on by the City Council. A current question was whether the Government's wine monopoly should be permitted to open a store in the town and whether a plebiscite should be taken.

An open vote in the City Council gave the dry forces more than two-thirds majority, but in a secret public plebiscite it was impossible to predict what the result might be. The debate was carried on with a certain dignity. Political parties as such took no official stand on the question, but the most eager representatives of the pros and cons wrote articles in the local newspapers. Most of the leaders of the Labour Party were dry, some fanatically so rather than from practical reasons.

The plebiscite was held and the wets won, but the City Council continued to deny the hotels licences to serve anything stronger than beer.

"A perfect solution," said our friend Bergenstick, "even though the opposite might have been better, since, then, we would have had more tourists in the hotels and fewer drunks in the streets."

It was a solution of sorts. There were other problems to be solved and Narvik had its share of them. Unemployment began to increase. We began to feel the world depression. Narvik was very much like a seismograph in that respect. All economic tremors were instantly felt on the payrolls. First, the Mining Company cut down on overtime and then explained the dismissal notices which were soon to follow. The years from 1932 to 1936 were the worst. During 1932 the average unemployment for organized labour in Norway stood at 30 per cent. It was going to rise almost to 40 per cent before it began to drop again in 1935.

D

The depression did not strike everywhere with the same force. Cities with small businesses and home production came through best. Narvik was hard hit but managed to struggle through without any real suffering. But, when the bottom was reached, both public and private resources were exhausted. Shops had gone bankrupt and house after house had been sold at auction, even though the same people continued to live in them.

For more than two years conditions were bad, with about one-third of the population partly or completely dependent upon public relief. The workers in the Swedish Iron Ore Company had agreed to work on a reduced time schedule in order to avoid further dismissals. The Ore Company itself operated under a tremendous deficit. The local income tax rose to 20 per cent, to which was added the State income tax. But there was no destitution. There was no want of food or clothing or fuel, and the people lived in the same houses as before. It was not regarded as fair to buy a house which had been taken over by the bank if the owner declared his intention of redeeming it.

It was not charity or private welfare that helped us through the crisis; it was law and justice. But we did engage in endless debates as to the form the assistance should take. The Conservatives pointed out the dangers in having the help come too easily. Something must be asked in return, it was said, if the people were not to lose their spirit and self-respect. A host of problems presented themselves. Should work be demanded in return for help? Should the assistance be in the form of cash, or in credit to be used for the purchase of the most necessary things? The last Conservative cabinet in Norway had even suggested that the acceptance of public help be coupled with the loss of certain civic rights. The opposite point of view, however, had the support of the people in the Labour movement and also of the majority of the Liberals.

We were face to face with a social crisis which affected individuals impartially. There was no question of blame or ill-will. It was bad enough to lose work and livelihood. To add shame to disaster would be too much. The unemployed had rights and should not be forced to stand as beggars before society. Society had the duty of aiding its members. The Gordian Knot lay in asking for work in return for help when there was not work enough to go around.

It was truly a paradoxical situation. A thousand tasks awaited accomplishment. Equipment stood idle and material lay waiting, with empty hands stretched toward them. Somewhere there had been a fatal weakness and resulting failure in the social and economic structure. We thought we knew where that weakness was, but it would take a long time to work it out. The immediate situation was that there was not enough work for everybody, and if people on relief were given regular jobs it would only mean that those already employed would lose theirs. We persisted, however, in the belief that assistance given should be looked upon as a loan from society, to be repaid when the opportunity came, a view which many on relief shared.

The fact that Norway did come through the crisis with comparative ease was due to the traditions behind Norwegian society. The social security apparatus functioned openly, so that everyone was able to understand the difficulties and follow the process. According to law, each town must see to it that no individual was without life's necessities, whether the needy had civic rights in that particular town or not. An intricate system of refunding rates had been established between the Government and the local authorities, but it was the responsibility of the individual towns and country communities to give needed help according to rates and regulations they themselves determined. In Narvik the rates were kept up, since they had to stand in reasonable relation to the level of living expenses in the town. In spite of all necessary reductions, the living standard of the town was higher than that of the coastal districts where the price of cod had dropped to a halfpenny a pound.

The expenses of the city rose steadily, and ability to meet them declined as fast.

On the surface all was peaceful—too peaceful. Few ships were in the harbour and there was little activity in the Iron Company.

V   *City Hall*

IN the midst of this period, to my complete surprise, I became Mayor
of the town. The old Mayor had worked in the city government
ever since the town had been established. Promotion had followed
promotion until now he had reached the highest civic position, that of
Supervisor of City Offices. As such, by law, he could not also retain the
office of Mayor.

Elections had been held in the autumn, and I had been elected to the
City Council as one of the twenty-four representatives of the Labour
Party. The new Council Members would not be inducted into Office
until after the first of the year, when the Mayor for the year would be
elected by the Council itself. Each of the different party groups nominated
its own candidate; but, as the Labour Party was strongest, its candidate
would be elected. A contest was expected between the railroad workers
and the company workers. There was always some rivalry between
them and meetings were often long and warm.

Just before the Party meeting opened a group of the older leaders
came to me and said that they had a plan that would simplify matters.
I was to be the next Mayor.

"But that is impossible. I am too young, too new up here." I could
think of many other reasons.

"Yes, but it is the simplest solution."

"Not for me," I answered.

The Party patriarch chewed a little.

"Well, men, we'd better begin the meeting," he said. Then to me,
"Now you do as we decide. We know that you aren't thirty yet, and that
you are a lawyer, and all sorts of things, but we will take the risk."

I was both a little angry and a little touched when the vote was cast and it became necessary for me to thank them for their confidence.

In the City Council itself there were no discussions. Each party nominated its own candidate, and then mathematics took over. I promised that I would do my best.

The City Council was elected for three years, a body of forty-four serious councilmen and women whose chief interest was to try to direct the city government as well as possible. They elected an Executive Council whose responsibility it was to conduct all current business. The Executive Council held weekly meetings, but the Mayor called together the entire City Council for discussion of vital issues and whenever the budget was to be prepared and voted on. The City Council controlled the Executive Council and also elected the representatives to the key committees. The machinery was rather slow-moving but it did its work smoothly and well. Not one penny of public funds could be misused. All economic measures were open to public inspection. There were heated debates and much waste of time in misunderstandings and delays, but we usually found our way to the proper solution of our problems. In any case, this was our public democratic government and this was the way we built our nation.

The situation was becoming desperate and it was imperative that the town have more money. The Railway and the Mining Company continued their dismissals, although they kept on the payrolls as long as possible the heads of families and those with long employment records. The young men were the first to go, and it was not pleasant to have to talk with these impatient boys and have nothing to tell them. They said that things could not continue longer in this manner. We agreed, but what was there to do? And yet there they stood, aggressive, forceful, eager, and at the same time willing to be reasonable.

"But we want work," they said. "You have been talking about a new hospital, about the school buildings that are overflowing, about the electric power plant that should be enlarged. The streets could be improved. The cliff down by the pier should be dynamited to straighten out the road. It has been planned for a long time. Why can't we begin now? The city is not finished. Can it not build and dynamite and improve and give us work?"

"Of course you are right," we answered. "There are many things that should be done. But we have no money. We are trying everything. Give us more time."

And they would retort, "Time is the one thing we have too much of now."

Our best did not seem to be enough, so we sent delegates south to see what could be done. The Conservative group appointed an able man. The Supervisor of City Offices had been down to borrow money before. The three of us travelled the route between Oslo and Stockholm again and again, and, finally, there were some tangible results. In Stockholm we made an arrangement with the Swedish Iron Ore Company that it should pay a minimum annual tax which in slump years would be looked upon as an advance tax payment on future profits. At the Government offices in Oslo we presented plans for new schools, a new hospital, and the expansion of the electric power plant. What we needed was money to pay for the necessary work. We were not able to secure assistance for our most ambitious plans, but the cliff by the pier was dynamited away.

When the Labour Party came into power with a National Cabinet we were on hand again with our appeals for help. We thought our friends were sadly cautious. But Narvik was not the only city hit by the depression. We concentrated on our request for the new hospital and we did receive a promise of money from the National Hospitalization Agency.

It was the Assistant Mayor who *personified* the new hospital. He was Chairman of the Board of the old hospital and for years had fought for expansion. Henry Ottemo was a stout and jovial railway carpenter, but he did not joke about the new hospital. It must be built of concrete and must adjoin the old wooden building, which would be changed into a nurses' home. He knew exactly how things should be. Mrs. Ottemo complained that her husband studied heavy books in bed every evening, books on dishwashing machines, innerspring mattresses, stainless steel, and floor finishing. At last the long-cherished dream was to become reality. In co-operation with the Head Surgeon he pressed the demands through the Government offices—but there never seemed to be enough money on hand. Finally, the Head Surgeon lent his personal savings to the project in order to meet the building expense and balance the account.

The Head Surgeon was one of the forceful personalities who made the poor little town so rich. He worked long hours year in and year out with no holidays other than lone Sunday ski trips in the mountains. Occasionally he permitted himself a "holiday" to work for some months in a hospital abroad. From one such trip he returned to tell us the seeming fairy tale of the Mayo Clinic somewhere out on the prairies of the American Middle West. He was a magnificent surgeon. As a private person he was a bachelor and very reserved, but within the limits of his reserved nature we were the best of friends. We passed many pleasant evenings in heated discussion of our seemingly divergent philosophies of life. At bottom, we were not too far apart, although he was in fundamental disagreement with my political views, perhaps mostly for the reason that they were those of the majority. It helped somewhat that he got his new hospital.

And then, gradually, things began to return to normal. People were buying again. It was no longer only the city which used money. More ships could be counted in the harbour. The reduction arrangement of working hours in the Iron Company was cancelled. The economic seismograph registered once more in the right direction. Things began to happen.

We began to build again, and building gave us deep satisfaction. We blasted mountains and hewed stone and fashioned dwellings for men. We altered the landscape for all time and impressed it with man's will. In form and colour we gave of ourselves.

I remember the long discussions we had with our old architect. When we outlined plans for a new chapel that was to stand on a hill near the churchyard north of the town, he said that at last he knew just what we wanted him to do—to remove one mountain and design a new one. We laughed. It may be that we had expressed ourselves in that way, but what probably had happened was that the mountains had affected us, and not we the mountains. We wanted something impressive and worthy of its purpose, combining strength and dignity with loveliness and charm. We built our little stone chapel and it looked not too different from the building we had planned. It really belonged on its hill overlooking the sea and the mountains. The town had a beautiful cemetery. We wanted to express our love for the living by our respect for the dead.

The next three or four years were going to be the happiest in the city's history. It was not a boom time, no one got wealthy—limited opportunities and high taxes prevented that—but it was a period of healthy economic growth. There were, alas, too many holes to be plugged before we could feel the real security of good times. The social machinery had broken down at certain points and repairs had to be made before we could proceed with expansion, but improvements continued to come into existence. We got our School Dental Clinic, and prepared complete blueprints for a great new school building of brick. Private business firms also recovered, although there remained the crying need for capital and, to some extent perhaps, for courage and imagination.

The proposal was made that we might offer assistance to a few Jewish business people in Germany and give them a second chance in Narvik. The two or three Jewish families we already had in town distinguished themselves in no other ways than by working a little harder and selling their goods a little cheaper than their competitors. A little imported cleverness and initiative might not hurt.

The problem came up for discussion in the City Council, the issue being whether this Jewish relief proposal should be dominated by political or humanitarian motives. It was voted to underwrite a recommendation for immigration and a working permit for a small business concern in Narvik, and to give active assistance in the form of cheap electric rates.

Some weeks later a middle-aged German Jew appeared. The situation in his own *Vaterland* was not entirely hopeless as yet, and he thought that the storm of anti-Semitism would abate as it had done so often before. But one could not be sure, since extremely ugly things had already happened in Nazi Germany. Through friends who had travelled in northern Norway he had heard of our hospitable town and had come to pay us a visit.

He was polite, but somehow suspicious. Both the people and the region appeared to him to be a little too reserved and he seemed to be seeking the reason. I do not know whether he understood us, that we had no ulterior motives, and that there was no absolute need for us to invite someone to build a little button factory on the empty lot next to the oil station on the pier. As for his race, we felt that it had certain characteristics which might be stimulating to our sedate way of life. Our offer was meant purely as an expression of sympathetic friendship. He expressed his gratitude and said that he would return to Germany to get his family, but we never saw him again.

We were not always successful in our youthful enthusiasm for personal initiative and the need for taking long chances. Too often, young, unemployed families which we sent farming, returned with the smallest potatoes in the world and huge indebtedness.

We were more successful with Mrs. Polly, the not exactly young but extremely ambitious owner of the Royal Hotel, the second largest hotel in town. Grand Hotel Phoenix was the largest, but its owner was not ambitious. Both were on the dilapidated side, that is the hotels. There were many complaints about the poor accommodation. Even the Grand had but one bath on each floor. The one on the ground floor leaked, and the one on the top floor was used by the proprietor himself, so it was only the one on the second floor that could really be used.

Mrs. Polly of the Royal sent us many letters, none of which resulted in money being placed at her disposal. Then Mrs. Polly visited us in person. She had had a new permanent wave and was brimming with enthusiasm and vitality. The tourist season was almost at hand. Would I not be interested in making it possible for foreigners to stay overnight in the town? Did not the city think it was high time to become a little more modern and up-to-date? Only the other day a real English baronet had come in on the train only to find that every room was taken. He had to sleep in the maid's room.

And the little blonde had to move out? I asked.

Well, that was the only objection the Baronet had voiced.

We laughed and went at the problem. It was, of course, to the city's interest that these conditions be improved, but how?

What if we built a truly Hotel Royal of concrete in functional architectural design, with baths and lifts, and a doorman in a burgundy uniform to match the draperies in the lobby?

And where would we secure the needed funds?

We might start a holding company.

But we would need money and good names.

All the merchants on Street 1 were interested.

Yes, but that didn't solve the problem of cash money. Even a holding company must have capital, at least to begin with.

Why not allocate public funds?

That idea was not especially new. Much Government money had already been invested in projects that seemed excellent, and yet the possibility of return in many cases was most uncertain. The inescapable result could only be that there would be criticism of the lack of business ability within the Administration.

Yes, but wasn't Narvik an exception? The Government had the Railway and had secured for itself an annual minimum income from the Swedish Iron Ore Company. Wasn't that so?

Well, we had ridden that horse for a long time, but we promised that we would try again. And so there was more pressure and more trips to the Capital. We had really begun to be experts in this line of business.

At Oslo I explained that, despite the alluring tourist advertising, the placards extolling the beauties of the Land of the Midnight Sun, there were no good hotels in that country. Tourists were invited and yet, when they arrived, they could not be offered proper sleeping accommodation. That this situation should exist in Narvik was especially unfortunate since it was the only town having railway connections with the continent. Once again the argument struck home.

A sort of semi-public co-operative was established within a framework of private capital. From the economic point of view the arrangement was rather complicated, but the new hotel that came into being was beautiful and simple. It had the undivided blessing of the town authorities and very limited liquor rights. The opening ceremonies were impressive, with moving speeches following the ice cream. Proper homage was paid to Mrs. Polly. Irritating incidents and grey hairs were forgotten. Madam was more blonde than ever. At last we were equipped to show our hospitality. Now the tourists could come.

And come they did, mostly from continental Europe. While they did not always have much money they did not lack enthusiasm.

Shipping increased. The Iron Ore Company worked night shifts during the dark season and the loading piers were bright under flood-lights. The Song of Work was heard between the mountains. Once more the world needed iron. Confidence has returned, the people said.

But most of the ships in the harbour flew red flags with a black swastika.

VI   *Lofoten*

LOCAL self-government has been a living reality in Norway since 1837. For a century it has educated the people to political maturity and social responsibility. Each township is so small and transparent that our democracy has become simple and direct. It may be, however, that this local colour in some respects tends to mark the borderlines a little too strongly.

In Narvik the people in the market place were as alert and disputatious in politics as the Greeks of ancient Athens. And the small but dignified town of Bodö was our Sparta.

Bodö was in reality a beautiful, idyllic town which could not help that it was centuries older than Narvik or that it was more fortunately situated in the direct line of communications along the outer coast. Bodö was the centre of civil and legal administration for the Northland. Here the civil authorities lived and here also were the higher courts.

Of course, as Mayor of Narvik, I must not express too high an opinion of little Bodö, which, after all, had not half the population of Narvik and had a Railway Committee which was one of our standing jokes. The committee was reorganized and somewhat rejuvenated every fourth year, but the good citizens of Narvik held that such changes might as well be made only once in twenty or fifty years, so slight was the probability that the railway would ever come to Bodö.

Back of this seemingly good-natured banter there was more than mere local rivalry. The feeling covered a sore spot in our local self-government system. The burdens did tend to become uneven. A new city with a socially and economically young citizenship had to carry burdens out of all proportion to its developed ability. As an example, the

Dröbak resort, with rich and pensioned skippers and merchants and few school children, could operate with a city income tax of 5 per cent, while in the industrial town of Narvik, where children were constantly being born, and where school buildings were always more or less crowded, it was necessary to make the tax about 20 per cent. A nation-wide system to even these differences in local taxation had been in the making for some time. Both in the Government itself and in the municipalities constructive forces were at work to correct the situation. And there were other points of difference, including the problems of communications.

These communication problems were not simple or easy to solve. For instance, there were the plans for land connections southwards. The plan for a highway from Narvik to Bodö had been in the blueprint stage long before my time. Bodö did have some road connection with the rest of the country to the south, but to the north there was no road continuation. Now certain misguided souls wanted to put through the highway over the islands and the outer fjord districts so that it would not pass through Narvik. We, on our side, argued that a highway must be built for the benefit of all the people and not only for tourists who wished to save petrol.

We held our meeting in the relatively neutral town of Svolvær. Shoemaker Pedersen of the Narvik City Council maintained that even the inhabitants of Bodö and Svolvær were reasonable human beings, and for this reason he had been given a seat on the communications committee where, it was felt, his illusions would be helpful or his eyes would be opened. The Narvik Chamber of Commerce was represented by Consul Mosling, who, as a burning local patriot, could be counted on to counterbalance Mr. Pedersen. The Mayors of the interested towns naturally would be called upon to present their arguments at the conference. We had chosen a week-end in February, a time when the Lofot fisheries were busiest.

Svolvær received us with a blanket of wet snow over streets deep in mud. Its position close to the ocean tended to make the climate warmer than in the inner fjord districts. Sunshine was breaking through for the first time after the long dark period. The fishing operations were going on in East Lofoten that year, which meant that the bulk of the fish was lying closer to the mainland. Svolvær harbour was packed with fishing boats. We saw them seeking land as we neared the harbour: big motorboats which carried the buyers, steamships with decks piled high with empty barrels for liver and roe, and thousands upon thousands of smaller craft, the whole an immense forest of ship masts.

A light fog had been half swept away by a breeze a sunset, but the horizon was still mysteriously diffuse. It looked as though the fishing fleet was sailing in from the very heavens themselves. The coughing of individual motors was drowned in the common symphony of all the motors of the fleet.

Svolvær harbour was different each time I saw it. In some respects there was more of personality and changing mood in that little harbour between the rugged mountains in Lofoten than in any other place I know in the world. The scene could change from one of sleepy-eyed intimacy to stark and brutal drama, but the over-all effect was always one of masculinity and virile strength. Its deepest essence was most clearly revealed in the nights of wintry hurricane roaring in from the sea. Just as the real feeling of the North is found in the long dark winter rather than in the light weeks of summer, so Lofoten is not a midsummer night's dream but rather a tower planted against storm, the Lofot Mountains defying a wild sea. From a distance the mountains appear impregnable, massive and solid in their great bulk; but, at closer view, narrow channels are visible between the rocky cliffs. Behind reefs and cliffs there are calm harbours. Such a place is Svolvær.

Tossing craft swing in around the breakwater from the storm-ridden Vestfjord and anchor in its calm. The pier is a handshale and the town extends into the water bidding all its welcome. Above the cluster of wooden houses stretches the tower of the simple stone church, standing as if on tiptoe. The church is the pride of Svolvær and during the winter is floodlighted and serves as a landmark.

It took some time before we found a free place at the pier, and darkness fell before we disembarked. The lanterns were lit on all the boats and thousands of lights were glowing. It was Saturday night and over the harbour there were accordions and singing and festive release.

As we had not arranged to meet until after the church service on Sunday, we sauntered around a while in the street from the pier to the market place. It was not cold, but the air was raw and it was more comfortable to keep in motion. The narrow street was packed with people, mostly young men in Sunday dress but for the heavy sea boots. Young girls chattered and threw their heads back in gay laughter. They were bareheaded, since they were out only to get some fresh air before bedtime. The cinema played brief but numerous showings of cowboy films filled with action. From within came the sound of the stamping of heavy boots, indicating that the hero had not come quickly enough to the rescue. But there were also other temptations. In the café windows were small placards, placed between the glass and the freshly ironed curtains: *Stewed Prunes With Cream*—3*d*. The fishermen, tired of the monotony of sandwiches, coffee, and canned milk, felt little compunction in spending their money for this delicacy.

In the street I met young Oscar. I knew he had been excused from the trade school in Narvik so that he might make enough money to finish his training as an electrician. We had been good friends since the previous summer, when he had been judged not guilty in a paternity case.

He had been almost too innocent when he explained, somewhat regretfully, to the court that he was not the guilty one. I had had a blood test made and this had saved him.

He told me that his fishing boat had been lucky and that his share might amount to twenty pounds.

"I suppose it's rather hard work?" I said.

"You mean the work out there at sea? Why, it's life itself!"

I invited him to have a glass of beer in the hotel, so that we might talk a while, but he asked to be excused. His clothes were filled with the smell of fish, so he had better keep out-of-doors. Besides, he had promised to take someone home. Well, good luck, and he must be careful, I told him. He couldn't expect that luck would always follow him.

"Oh, I have it in the blood, you know," he said as he went on his way.

When I reached the hotel, most of the delegates had arrived, and we had a pleasant social evening. After all, there were many other problems in life than extending the highway down to little Bodö.

The hotel was built with one of its wings along the pier and the lights in the harbour could be seen from the windows. The smell of fish was almost as strong within as without. It was not of the fragrance of flowers, but it was an honest and decent smell and it somehow belonged there. After all, it was the proper smell for the season.

We heard the groaning of the sea. The radio had warned of storm. The day of rest to-morrow would spare lives. Perhaps the storm would have abated when work began once more. We could see the forest of masts waving to and fro even in the calm of the harbour. The moon sailed through torn skies and sharpened the contours of the mountain at the back of the town. Snow still remained at the mountain top giving a white background to the strange stone formation halfway up the slope. When seen from the harbour, this silhouette resembled the horns of a monstrous animal head which the fishermen called the Svolvær Goat. But the townspeople, who saw it from another side, explained to tourists that it was the Two Lovers who had stood there in stone since sin came into the world.

After general handshaking we sat down in the bar-room around glasses. It was only natural that Lofot stories were told, stories of smart buyers outsmarted by still smarter fishermen.

A fish buyer from Kabelvåg began to tell about Draugen and the superstition among fishermen. Draugen was Death in the Sea, the scream from overturned lifeboats. Admittedly, very few could give a description of him, since Draugen sounded the last warning before the boat plunged into the depths. It had, however, happened that some had cheated him, and that half-drowned men had sometimes ridden overturned boats to safety. But such lucky fellows usually had little to tell. Perhaps, after a long period, they would talk, but then one could not tell how much to believe.

It was certain that Draugen was no shipmate to sit with on a capsized skiff. He wore oilskins like an ordinary fisherman, but his death-like skull shone in phosphorescent green, his eye sockets were empty, and his voice was the screech of an owl.

"You don't mean to tell me that people still believe in such things?" I asked.

"Oh, no, not any more. Since people began to use motorboats they have not talked very much about Draugen."

"You mean to say the people have become more modern together with their equipment?"

"Well, Draugen does not like the exhaust of the motors."

We laughed, and the conversation turned to the question of state subsidy to the fisheries. All other Norwegian industries had achieved a certain degree of security, some with, some without, assistance from the Government. But fishing, the most Norwegian of them all, still laboured under great difficulties. When fishing was poor, the fishermen barely met the expenses of tackle and equipment, and, when it was good, wholesale prices were forced so low that there was little profit. In recent years the Government had stepped in. The possibility of speculation was restricted, subsidies were provided for the purchase of tackle, and the export trade was made subject to regulation.

"The fishermen, too, must be organized," said an official of the Bureau of Fisheries who had taken part in the discussion. "That is the only way the living standards can be raised. It is slow, and it is not easy so far as the Lofot fishermen are concerned. People organize more quickly where they are permanently settled. But here they come from all parts of the country, they fish all over the Lofot Sea, and sell their catch at whichever harbour happens to be closest. The Government wants to see them organized, and it is certainly possible to bring it about."

"But what will happen to us poor fish buyers?" the fish merchant from Kabelvåg inquired.

"Perhaps you will have to exert yourselves a little," the official replied.

We smiled, but the man from Kabelvåg did not think it funny. He replied with irony.

"So you can even make politics out of herring and cod!" he said.

The conversation turned to the international political situation. The men were well informed and had followed with anxiety the insane developments in Germany, which they thought a kind of political epidemic. It had broken out in Italy first and there it might have been stopped. Was it not true that the League of Nations had protested against the Fascist rape of Ethiopia? And, even though the League of Nations had little power, it still had a weapon in the form of sanctions, a weapon it had declared its willingness to use. As things stood, we in Norway took the economic sanctions seriously and paid dearly for it. Thousands of tons of fish which otherwise would have been sold to Italy were left lying to rot when the trade stopped because we strictly observed the appeal not to buy Italian goods. Had the Great Powers shown similar good faith in action, the whole catastrophe might have been averted.

"But why have you always been against military preparedness?" Kabelvåg was again on the offensive.

I felt it my turn to answer.

"The idea has been that the first world war should have been the absolutely final war. Groups have been at work in all countries to make this dream a reality. And these liberal groups and the different labour organizations the world over were really a guarantee that the peace would be kept. But, when the German democracy and the German labour movement were crushed, this basis for international peace disappeared. We realized that this approach was destroyed, and said so. We are now all agreed that we must strengthen our national defences. The defence problem is no longer a political question. And the defence budget we have to-day is the largest in our history."

"Perhaps it is too late. Up here anyone may come and take us over."

Here I received assistance.

"These naked mountains up in the North? Who could possibly be interested in them? The struggle for life is so severe that certainly no one could possibly envy us. And how would they get here in the first place? There are no communications except by the ocean."

"They'd better wait until we've built that new highway."

"And about that we will fight tomorrow," said Bodö, as we rose from the table.

The highway meeting was not so bad after all. At least we did agree that there were several alternative routes possible. And, in the end, the Government would have to decide where the road was to go. Each of the committees felt that there would certainly be no question as to which was the most sensible route.

VII *The Gulls Fly Low*

BACK in Narvik, we continued to talk about the crisis. It was an old habit. The true picture of the situation, however, was that we were enjoying the best period the town had ever experienced. The change had come gradually and was reflected in life and work even more than in mere money and high prices. Once more iron had become a precious metal.

Out in the yellow-painted house at Framnes we had almost all we could desire. At last even a little daughter arrived. We called her Siri.

Otherwise not much happened. The steady flow of days passed quietly and happily with pleasurable activity, their similarity serving only to fill the weeks and months with more contentment. The City Gardener planted flowers in the Market Place and the people did not disturb them. We loved life and the town and our country, and thought it perfectly natural that tourists should come to see its glories. Not all the tourists were the most desirable, and they often had little cash; still, they were foreigners and added colour to our existence.

At intervals some rather curious individuals came to town. In the late autumn, the mad Major Vidkun Quisling arrived on a visit. He had just resigned from active military service to devote himself to his philosophical and political studies and was to give a lecture in the Temperance Hall.

A rather large group attended. It had been a long time since a circus had been in town.

The speaker was late, giving us an opportunity to refresh our memories of his strange career. What one did not recall, his neighbour would relate as we sat on the hard wooden benches waiting for the show to begin.

After the last war he had been the Norwegian military attaché in

Moscow. He accompanied Nansen on his travels through the hunger districts and returned home at length with an anti-capitalistic point of view and a collection of antique Russian paintings, which he tried to sell through a Jewish art dealer with whom he was to have a long legal feud concerning the dealer's share. Major Quisling put his ideas at the disposal of the Labour Party and offered to organize Red Guards. When he was ignored by the Left he veered to the Right, where he had considerably more success.

Quisling was Minister for Defence in the most reactionary Cabinet the country has ever had, an Agrarian Cabinet in the years 1931–1933. During this period he distinguished himself chiefly by being the victim of a nocturnal attack which was said to have been perpetrated upon him one night when he was alone in the Defence Ministry. We could not make much sense out of his story that an invisible Bolshevik had thrown pepper in his face and hit him from behind with a blunt instrument, with the result that he had fainted. Thanks to his strong physical constitution, he had lost neither life nor military secrets. He never succeeded in apprehending the assailant, but he did discover several points to add to his propaganda against the Labour movement. At length he severed all connection with the Agrarian Party and for a brief period acted the lone, strong man, until he attempted to stage a political comeback by means of his own newly-created but hopelessly unpopular party "National Unity."

This was the "Pepper Minister," to hear whom we had paid sixpence. It was not worth more. The only qualification he seemed to possess for the role of dictator and *Führer* of the Norse race was a doughy face and a complete lack of humour. It certainly could not be said that he did not take himself or life seriously. He began by predicting the bankruptcy of the British Empire and proceeded to bury international Jewish capitalism together with the rotten democratic system of government. As for the Norwegian people, there was still hope, not because of any intelligence or self-control they had thus far shown, but because of racial qualities in the national character. As yet, he said, we were still raving in the night of liberalism, but before too long the strong, clear day was sure to come.

We shook our heads and went for a stroll in Street 1, to clear our minds in the fresh evening air. That paranoiac could thank the "night of liberalism" that he still was permitted to be loose. Probably not a single person in the audience really agreed with him.

We knew that he was publishing a weekly in Oslo and that he had small groups of adherents here and there in the country. The movement was without any political significance. It was a "defiance phenomenon"

which, in difficult times, might fill a certain psychological need, but it
was without any positive content. The "leaders" of National Unity
were superannuated crackpots that the world had not appreciated. The
"followers," such as they were, consisted of unmarried women of the
critical age, and discontented youth without work. Two or three years
earlier, when unemployment had been at its peak, Quisling had enjoyed
his greatest vogue and had managed to poll between one and two per
cent of the votes in the National election. Afterwards he had been on the
down grade as the depression abated and life again became more normal.
The minute Communist Party had a similar experience, even though it
had more to offer than the Quisling group.

Once again we began to believe that life was not too complicated and
that "normal" times really were the normal way of life. At intervals
we had tremors of doubt; but, as long as one's wishful thinking and one's
immediate environment approximately agreed, it was tempting to believe
and act accordingly.

Iron ore passed steadily through the town. Work at the piers went on
day and night; three steamers were loaded simultaneously, while others
lay waiting their turn in the harbour. Never had so much iron ore been
shipped in the Ofotfjord as during that winter. But the local newspapers
no longer printed poems about iron being made into plough-shares and
building materials.

We still counted the ships in the harbour every morning and automati-
cally added the three by the pier, but there was not the same unmixed
joy as before in watching the feverish activity.

Austria, Sudetenland, Czechoslovakia—with each annexation the iron-
ore flow through the town assumed a darker and more sinister hue. But
we told ourselves that we were without guilt. It was not our iron. We
had no power over it. And anyway, what could we do?

The summer light returned, and with it our faith in beauty and life.
Once more foreign guests came to admire our country and reservations
had to be made far in advance for berths on the coastal steamers.

Later, we often discussed how strangely different the tourist traffic had
been during that last summer. Could it be that the events themselves cast
shadows backwards in our memory? No, there had been a definite and
observable difference.

The German summer tourists of 1939 actually had money. The visitors
were no longer young boys who tramped about with their songs and
mandolins. Neither were they the usual grasshopper swarm from the
Kraft durch Freude boats, those "tourists" who used to come ashore with
wurst sandwiches, and who bought post cards and soap. The new German
tourists travelled first class and did not haggle over prices. They were

mostly younger and middle-aged men of erect carriage who really knew
how to appreciate our country's natural beauty, through fine telescopes.
They seemed very studious about it.

In the late summer we were travelling, a party of lawyers and the
District Judge, on the northbound express steamer. We were returning
from a court session at Bodö. A party of German tourists was on board,
including a widely-travelled and convivial *Herr Doktor* and his wife. The
couple used every opportunity to gather small groups around the coffee
table in the saloon to discuss German culture and intellectual life.

The Germany that had created Beethoven and Goethe was appealing
to the land of Henrik Ibsen and Edvard Grieg. The German people were
extending their open hand; why were we withholding ours?

We explained in equally friendly and polite terms that we had never
harboured any dislike for the old German culture. We had believed in
the Weimar Republic and we had shown our sympathy in many ways,
but we did not understand the New Order. We hated brutality and
intolerance.

The Doctor moved back in his easy chair. He must have answered
similar remarks before.

No, it might be true that we did not know too much about the New
Germany. Actually there had not been much brutality and violence.
There had been only a few skirmishes with certain cliques of Jews and
Bolsheviks, who had failed to realize that the German people had lost
patience with them. Since we in Norway did not have such problems, it
was only natural that we did not understand them. The Jews had multiplied like rabbits. They had taken over one industry or trade after another.
The Bolsheviks had undermined public morals. The politicians had
done nothing but talk and intrigue. The German nation had decided to
determine its own destiny. Personally, the *Führer* loathed any use of
violence. His only aim was to create order. He wanted peace and progress.
The New Germany was filled with song and work. The people breathed
a purer air. Unemployment was a thing of the dark past. Culture and
intellectual life were blooming.

When the Doctor ran out of breath his wife took over. Their enthusiasm was genuine enough.

We were polite and reserved, but curious. We admitted that we had
not heard much about the intellectual life in the New Germany. The
round and amiable Norwegian judge asked whether the lady could tell
us a little about the new German authors. The New Order most certainly
must have inspired new artists. In our own national history each epoch
had its great names. Ibsen and Björnson had received State pensions in
recognition of their work. How was it in Germany?

The question was innocent and without malice, but the faces of the Doctor and his wife became red and taut.

No, he did not mean those who sat in. . . . The distressed Judge realized that he had again got off on the wrong foot and attempted to right matters.

He had only wished to ask the lady to tell a little about the new German literature.

The Doctor interrupted. He had regained his best bedside manner.

The gentlemen must understand that the New Germany as yet was so much in its infancy that it had not advanced so far as the matter of books . . . the writing of books, he corrected himself. The new literature would come when Germany was ready, after other important matters had been settled.

The Judge smiled with relief and we went on with our coffee.

The printed Nazi propaganda met with still less success in Norway. Through the post we received pamphlets and circular letters containing simply-explained racial theories combined with flattering invitations to join in Nordic cultural fellowship.

We knew *one* thing, that Nazism was violence and oppression. Our periodicals had carried excellent analyses of the Nazi violence mentality that had created a machine which no one could stop, least of all its inventors.

And still we did not believe in a possible war, at least not in a war that would affect our national future. To play safe, however, additional funds were voted for national defence and the Government got without question whatever it requested. We were willing to pay fire insurance premiums according to traditional rates, but we did not believe that our own house would ever burn. We were out of the traffic, and mountains and greystone did not seem inflammable.

Nor did we believe in any danger from the East. Russia had her own ice-free harbours in the North. We were not immediate neighbours. Finland drove her narrow corridor between us. We had never been at war with Russia. The danger from the south was greater, but there was, thank God, an ocean between us and Hitler. We believed that we had good reason to feel fairly secure, especially since we were paying such extremely high taxes.

The Russian-German Pact came as a shock and the war as a tragedy that might have been prevented, although we did not know exactly how. Taxes continued to rise and placards were posted on public buildings warning us to be cautious and to keep silent. We began to doubt whether we really had very much to keep silent about.

Over the New Year holiday I went to Oslo in connection with the building of our new school. I found that all my old anti-militaristic friends had become interventionists in principle, if it could be said that any principles were sharply defined any more. All political matters had become inextricably tangled. We found ourselves on the same side as British imperialism. During the last months we had all helped to organize assistance for the Finnish people in their fight against the dream of our young days. It was certainly not easy any longer to see clearly either the principles or the lines. It appeared that we would have to build a new world view from the bottom up, to begin again with the simple and basic moral values like truth and justice, freedom and mutual consideration. In our University days we had turned fine phrases to the effect that each generation must fight for its freedom anew. It now appeared that the phrases were going to be given very literal application.

When I returned to Narvik I learned that our Head Surgeon had volunteered at a frontline military hospital in Finland and that the Chief of Police had arrested the local representative of the Krupp Works. Engineer Möller was a spy. With German thoroughness he had kept a diary which showed that reports had been transmitted to a German centre in Stockholm concerning the sailing dates of British iron-ore transports. Some of them had disappeared without a trace out in the ocean.

A German fish buyer had spent the winter in Narvik. Herr Koehln travelled all over the coast and we were convinced that he was also a spy, but the police were unable to get any evidence. The German Consul, Wusof, who lived at the Grand Hotel, was protected by his position. Mr. Gibbs, the British Consul, lived at the Royal. To people who insisted that all foreign consulates are equally evil in wartime, we pointed to these two men. The German Consul nosed about everywhere and invited as many people as possible to his table in order to learn Norwegian and Norwegian customs. Mr. Gibbs and his secretaries went back and forth to their offices with clock-like regularity and knew scarcely enough Norwegian to say *Skål*, not because they did not wish to talk to us, but because they did not wish to appear indiscreet.

On Christmas Eve Madame Polly gave a party to which the Finnish refugee children in the town and vicinity were invited. She was dressed and decorated in her best style. The Christmas tree itself was locked in an adjoining room until after dinner, when Consul Gibbs played Santa Claus, even though he refused to dress for the part. The whole city had sent gifts. It was a sad joy. Some of the Finnish children were accompanied by their mothers or older relatives, but few of them spoke anything but Finnish. We could not understand one another, the children were shy, and the mothers were tired, but the food and the sweets seemed to be enjoyed.

This year the winter darkness was more burdensome than usual. There were heavy snowfalls and the winter storms seemed never to end. The express steamers were as much as a whole day late and the local steamers frequently had to leave without making connections or getting the mail.

The sombre atmosphere in the harbour grew ever more depressing. The ore boats lay waiting even after they had been loaded, as if they hesitated to go into the open sea. Then, usually on moonless nights, they would suddenly disappear, one nationality at a time.

Before the war the annual ore export had averaged between four and seven million tons. Two thirds of it had gone to Germany. Now, more British than German flags were to be seen. The Norwegian coast had many open stretches and the Germans evidently feared for their ships. The Swedish ore port of Luleå in the Baltic is frozen until late May, and the major part of the Swedish ore had always gone out of Narvik. When we met with the Swedes in conferences on taxation or labour problems they often chided us that we must not imagine ourselves indispensable to the ore export. Plans were afoot for the building of new icebreakers that would keep Luleå harbour open during the winter. It might even become feasible to transport the ore by rail to the harbours in southern Sweden. On such occasions we expressed a certain ironical gratitude over the fact that our beloved brother nation preferred to keep our workers occupied rather than their own. We knew that our position was fairly secure. The good Lord had in his inscrutable wisdom put the ore on the other side of the border but he had left the key on the outside. We had the *harbour*. From an economic point of view it would not be practicable to export the ore any other way, all the year round, nor was it technically probable. We had always been proud of the fortunate location of our harbour. Now we began to wonder whether, after all, we were so fortunate.

Steamers flying the flags of the belligerent nations lay side by side. In times like these the crews were forbidden to go ashore, but occasionally it happened that men did leave the ships.

One day in February I received an unexpected visitor. It was on the ninth, the day of the first return of the sun at the end of the winter darkness. The schools were closed, and the community had declared a local though unofficial holiday. The streets were crowded with people, their faces turned toward the sun. It rose in its full size above the mountains, leaned for a minute against the crooked nose of the Sleeping Queen, and floated free a moment before it sank, seemingly tired after its exertion.

From my own office I had just phoned the City Hall.

No, there was no post to-day. It was really very quiet this morning.

Most of the clerks had gone into town on some important business or other.

I smiled as I hung up. Truly, the sun shone alike on the just and the unjust.

The secretary announced that a young man wished a private interview. He was German but easy to understand, she said, with pride in her linguistic ability.

He was very young, barely twenty. He took a seat in the client's chair across my desk.

No, he had not come on any legal affair. But he wanted first to know whether he might speak freely.

Of course, I said.

He had been given my name by some social democrat friends in Germany. As I would know they were still active there. He had been put on duty aboard one of the ore steamers, but this was to be his last trip. On his return to Germany he would be drafted into the army, but he did not believe in this war. He refused to sacrifice his life to Hitler. He intended to desert his ship here in Narvik.

I asked him for his papers.

That was exactly where the hitch came in. He had neither identification papers nor passport. He would like to hear my position in the matter. What were the Norwegian Government agencies likely to do with him?

I told him that he probably would be returned to his ship immediately. As he must realize, crew members from belligerent ships were not permitted ashore.

Yes, he knew that. He had sneaked ashore to meet me. It might be possible that he could get back without detection. But, if he were to stay ashore, would he run the risk of being given up?

It was no easy matter. As he must understand, we on our side had to show some caution. We were neutral.

But others had entered the country.

Only too well I knew that to be a fact. There were many Germans in the country. In earlier days we had welcomed the *Wandervögel* and tourists; now we had refugees, most of them without papers. Not long ago another man had deserted his ship. He had told me that he was an Austrian trade union official. His story was plausible. When the *Anschluss* broke in on his beloved Vienna, he had been discovered attempting to hide the trade union treasure, and had been put in a concentration camp. He had managed to escape, and had worked himself north to a Baltic port where friends had smuggled him on board a freighter bound for Narvik. We gave him money and bought him a ticket to Trondheim.

He had been invited by a student club to participate in a discussion on socialism and the modern labour movement. He had not shown much knowledge of the subject and when, later, he was discovered to be taking an undue interest in the harbour works of Trondheim, he was arrested as a spy.

I related this incident to my new guest. He blushed, but looked me straight in the eye and assured me that he was no Nazi, that he had come this distance to be with a truly free people. He wanted my advice.

I called the Chief of Police. He said that he had orders to arrest all aliens without papers.

But if it concerns a German sailor who refuses to fight Hitler's war? Would he be returned to his ship?

Hmmmn.

From his voice I could almost visualize our humane Chief of Police scratching his head.

We must be careful, of course. We had run into trouble already. Political prisoners were not supposed to be given up. Each case must be decided strictly on its own merit. He could not make any statement beforehand.

I repeated his answer to the German youth. He did not seem to be entirely satisfied, but he thanked me and reassured me of his admiration for the free Norwegian people.

Perhaps we might meet again.

We should.

During February and March we enjoyed some bright, quiet weeks. The latter part of the winter was usually calm. March was the best month for ski-ing. The mountains were a fairyland of light and the snow was heavy with ice crystals, ideal for sliding. Then the grey weather began to drift in from the ocean. The fishing ended in April and the spring storms were at the door. Even the sea birds sought shelter.

"It is a sure omen of storm," the fishermen said, "when the sea gulls fly low."

VIII *The Ninth of April*

THE ninth of April was a Tuesday. That day the lightning struck and our world broke in pieces. It cannot be said that it came without warning. We had seen the storm growing on the horizon but we had not realized that it would hit even us. We had had omens, but we had not interpreted them.

Afterwards we often talked of the day before the catastrophe. Dogs howl on many dark nights, but it is only after death has visited a house that the howls assume significance. Perhaps we recalled the day only because it was the last in a normal world.

Monday, as usual, had brought two days' mail from the South, and there had been the regular busy tempo in the office. I was interrupted by a telephone call from the harbour. A British sea captain asked me to come down with a certificate of seaworthiness for the freighter S.S. *Romanby*. There had been a minor collision in the harbour the week before. I represented Lloyd's of London and had arranged the details in connection with the repairs.

On the way I met a friend from the Customs Office. He had worked all night and was on his way home. A total of twenty-five iron-ore ships filled the harbour, roadstead and piers. All had been inspected on arrival and their radio transmitters had been sealed. That morning a huge whaling ship, the *Jan Wellem*, had arrived from the north. He had been on board himself. It had exceptionally large food stores for being southward bound. Perhaps it had been chased into harbour by the British. He had not noticed anything unusual. The crew had been polite, but the cigars were bad.

I told him that I was going on board a British ship.

"Then you will at least get better cigars," he yawned, and was on way.

I was taken to the ship by a ferryman who operated a kind of harbour taxi service.

Business was not too bad. Tips were better since there were more British and fewer Germans, but there was not much of the traditional good spirit in the harbour. Everything was secretive. No one knew when the boats arrived or left. On the surface everything was peaceful. The ships lay side by side, flying the Union Jack or the Swastika, but they all had secret machines covered up on the foredeck. They kept their cannons under cover. Harbour police were to be seen on every side. There was much talk about spies, yet no one had been arrested since Möller, so things could not be so bad after all. But it was not pleasant any more.

Aboard the S.S. *Romanby* I was invited to the Captain's cabin after we had inspected the repairs. He poured drinks.

"*Skål for Narvik*," said the skipper by way of a toast. "You see I have already learned some Norwegian."

"And an essential part of it," I answered.

I gave the Captain his certificate and we sat down for a little farewell chat. We talked about the strange war and about Narvik.

"When things begin to happen will we be likely to get into trouble?" I asked.

The Captain quieted my fears.

"So far Great Britain has, perhaps, not done too much in the land fighting," he said, "but she still rules the sea. A freighter or two the Nazis might be able to sneak up along your neutral coast to Narvik, but warships which have to go out to sea will not get through. You may rest assured, there is no danger up here."

As I left I observed the huge Nazi whaling ship, *Jan Wellem*, riding at anchor at some distance. An oversized swastika flew from the foremast. A little farther off lay the Norwegian *panzer* boats *Norge* and *Eidsvold*.

After office hours Ellen came to meet me. We were going to the cinema. The official radio news bulletin was broadcast in the theatre at 7 p.m. The news report that evening was that the wreckage of a German transport, the *Rio de Janeiro*, had drifted ashore earlier in the day on the coast of southern Norway. With the wreckage were dead horses and drowned soldiers. The soldiers all appeared to have been young men and of the same year classes. There was no official comment.

Afterwards we had supper at the Hotel Royal, where we visited Mrs. Polly. She told us that some of the harbour officials had also been in for supper, but when they heard the seven o'clock news, they had hurriedly left for the harbour. The officers and crew on the Norwegian *panzer* boats were all held on board, no leaves even permitted. Several foreign journalists were staying at the hotel, two Americans and the English newspaper man, Giles Romilly, a nephew of Mr. Churchill. They had sat in the telephone booth all the evening. The incident of the sunk German transport must have meant something, but no one seemed to know exactly what. Could it mean an attack on Great Britain?

We continued to talk war on the way home.

I repeated what the British sea captain had told me earlier in the day. Up here nothing could happen.

Before we put out the lights we went in to see Siri. She had, as usual, kicked off her covers and was sleeping peacefully in the least comfortable position. This night she had her head underneath her pillow in sweet company with Trine, the faithful but legless old doll.

Early the next morning we were awakened by a terrific blast. The whole house rocked. Ellen jumped up. What was it?

I said it was probably dynamiting down on the Iron Company grounds. It was 4.45 a.m. We'd better try to sleep some more.

Then came an even more terrifying explosion. The windows rattled.

"That's not from the Company, that's from the sea!"

I did not answer, but ran to the window and raised the curtains. The dawn was heavy with fog, and through it we saw tongues of flames. There was shooting in the harbour.

"Is it war?"

"It can't have anything to do with us," I said. "Some German ships must have been chased into the fjord by the British."

Then there was a new sea of fire and a tremendous explosion. We felt it rather than saw it.

Siri was stirring in her room. We heard her climbing over the bed rail. Then the tripping of small bare feet over the floor. She stood in the door.

"What is it?" And, as we didn't answer, "Is it Christmas?"

We had told her that there would be fireworks from the ships in the harbour on Christmas Eve.

Faces appeared in all the open windows. We shouted to one another. No one knew what it might be. A soldier came running from the guard post out on the peninsula.

No, he didn't know for sure. Too much fog. They could not see. But the harbour had reported that the shooting came from the Germans.

We dressed and went downstairs.

Germans shooting! We could not understand it.

We talked with the next-door neighbours, who were also dressed.

How many soldiers did we have in town?

Not very many, it seemed. But inland, to the north of the fjord, there was Elvegård training field, and there were some five hundred men there.

It took some minutes to quiet Ellen and Siri before I ran down into the town.

At the bridge there was a great number of Nazi soldiers. They had mounted their machine guns.

People filled the streets. They said the city had capitulated.

Capitulated, what nonsense!

But the German flag flies in the Market Place.

That was correct. A huge flag was flying over the Telegraph Building. I ran to the City Hall. A swastika flew there also. In the City Council room I found the caretaker. He said he had witnessed a strange performance in the Market Place a few minutes earlier. Hundreds of Germans had marched up from the piers and had hustled the Norwegian soldiers together in the Market Place. Then Colonel Sundlo and the Norwegian forces had marched over to the school on the other side of the town. But some of the Norwegian officers and half of the soldiers had fallen out of the lines before they reached the bridge and had gone up the street leading towards the Railway Station. He had heard rifle shots from that direction. It appeared that Sundlo had surrendered his men and had ordered them to their quarters. Obviously, some of them had refused to obey the order and had bolted.

Later, German soldiers had arrived at the City Hall and had hoisted their flag on the mast. Both Grand and Royal Hotels were swarming with German officers. The Telegraph Office and the Railway Station were occupied. Further, he had nothing to report. Would there be office hours as usual?

Yes, usual office hours.

In the meantime the first office workers had appeared. I asked them to call all the members of the City Council, as well as the leaders of the most important institutions, the Railway, the Iron Company, the Hospital, and the Telegraph Office. I also asked them to try to contact Colonel Sundlo, so that we might become oriented and decide what action to take.

From the corner windows of the City Hall we saw German soldiers hurrying about in all directions. They evidently knew what they were to do. They carried all kinds of strange weapons, and hand grenades dangled about their bodies as though they were walking Christmas trees.

The Hospital reported. It was packed with dead and wounded Norwegian navy boys and some Germans. Both the Norwegian warships had been sunk. It appeared that all the Norwegian Navy officers had been killed. The Commander-in-Chief of the local sea defences, Per Askim, had just been brought in on a truck. They did not know whether he was alive.

Some Norwegian sailors had said that there had been five hundred men aboard the Norwegian men-of-war. Most of them must have been killed in the first half-hour. The *Eidsvold* had stopped the German destroyer outside the harbour. A German officer in a motor launch had come over to arbitrate. He had demanded immediate and complete surrender. Captain Willoch of the *Eidsvold* had radiophoned the demand to Commander Askim on the *Norge*. He had replied, "We will not surrender. We will fight."

The German officer had been given safe return passage; but, before he reached his ship, he had signalled the Norwegian decision by the means of a flash-pistol. Then torpedoes came out of the fog. Without having opportunity to fire a shot the *Eidsvold* was blown up in a single terrific explosion. Eight men were saved, no officers.

The survivors from the *Norge* reported that they had had warning a few hours earlier that a German naval squadron was steaming from the ocean into the fjord. The *Norge* had cleared the decks for action and had her 21-centimeter cannons in readiness. The first vague shadows that appeared in the harbour opening had been attacked immediately, but the heavy fog blanket prevented definite aim. A second later the fog hid the opposing forces from each other. Aboard the *Norge* they realized that several enemy ships had already entered the harbour. One of these was next sighted alongside the steamship pier. The *Norge* opened fire but was hit herself by German torpedoes coming in from all directions. She sank within twenty seconds.

The Railway Station reported that two trains had left for Sweden early in the morning, but the line had been disrupted. The ferries still operated. From both sides of the Narvik peninsula people were trying to get out of town.

Now the members of the City Council began to appear. We sat down at the long table with the green cover. Few words were spoken. The faces were ashen grey. We realized that something terrible had happened. We understood and yet could not understand. The military must have some information. We had better wait.

A sudden noise came from the staircase. There were calls for the Chief of Police and myself. We were to be escorted to the German Headquarters. The Chief of Police entered the room and we left together. At the main entrance German soldiers stood waiting for us. They were ridiculously erect. We were to come to the Grand Hotel.

Why exactly to the Grand? I thought.

The lobby was filled with German Officers, most of them young. Consul Wusof steamed about, busy as a bee, his hands full of documents. He took time to explain to us that the General would soon arrive and that

it would be his pleasure to introduce us to Lieutenant-General Edward
Dietl.

"This is a very extraordinary situation, Mr. Mayor. The events took
even me by complete surprise."

The Consul beamed an exalted smile and waved his documents.

Then you have been exceedingly fast on your typewriter, you devil,
I thought, but we only sat down to wait.

Soon the General arrived in a taxi. Everybody stiffened a bit more.
We were presented to him, and the General began to talk. He was tall,
with a narrow, sharp face and a slight stoop. A lieutenant tried to attract
his attention; he had a Norwegian at his back.

"What is it?"

"It's only the cab driver who says the General did not pay his fare.
We haven't got small Norwegian change, Herr General."

"Scandalous!"

The General was extremely apologetic for this oversight. The Chief of
Police and I exchanged glances. They had murdered our navy boys in
the harbour and had occupied our town, and now they apologized because
they lacked change.

"Only an oversight, Herr Mayor."

We nodded.

The General was politeness itself.

"Let us hope we shall have more time later. We have just arrived.
I want to make it clear from the start that we have come as friends, to
protect your country against any further British breaks of your neutrality.
The German *Wehrmacht* has taken over the protection of Oslo, Bergen,
and Trondheim. We have encountered no armed resistance anywhere."

"But our navy men in the harbour?"

"Sad, isn't it?"

We did not answer.

"I can assure you, gentlemen, that we do not wish any bloodshed.
I am happy to inform you that Norway is now occupied peacefully
in the name of *Der Führer*."

I looked towards the Chief of Police. He shrugged his shoulders in
dismay, indicating that I should answer.

"We are not prepared to discuss the destiny of our nation with the
General. Perhaps we should limit ourselves to our own town here?"

"Well, your Colonel showed good sense in not offering any resistance.
He surrendered the city to me. As Commander-in-Chief of the occupation
troops I am now in charge. I wish, however, to make it clear that the
Civil Administration must continue as heretofore, at least insofar as it is
in keeping with military expediency. We need a certain control of com-

munications, and, for their own protection, the populace must be indoors at 8 p.m. That should be all. No, not quite, my troops need some shaving cream and similar articles. You must inform the local business people that they must accept German currency. To simplify matters, we have printed special reichsmarks. They are worth, let me see——"

The General examined some documents brought to him by his adjutant.

"Here it is. One reichsmark equals one krone and sixty öre. I think this will do for the present. I will be happy to see the gentlemen at a later occasion."

The General made a bow and turned to his staff. We were made to understand that we might go.

At the City Hall the officials were expecting us, Colonel Sundlo among them. No words seemed to have been uttered.

I told what I knew and reported on my conference with the German General. First we must try to get an idea of where we stood, and then concentrate on the tasks nearest at hand.

Colonel Sundlo had better give his explanation first. The Colonel was calm and impassive.

He could say only that he had been taken completely by surprise when the attack came and that he had found it useless to resist after the Norwegian warships had been sunk. He had from three to four hundred men ashore. The Germans were said to have ten thousand.

Had he contacted his superiors?

Yes, in the midst of the attack he had talked by telephone with the Headquarters at Harstad.

Had he received power to surrender the town?

Yes. Well—one might say that that question had been left somewhat at his own discretion. He wished to add, on his own behalf, that it seemed that the Norwegian military authorities did not completely understand the situation.

But what of the rest of the country?

It would appear that the leading cities in the southern part of the country had been taken. It was hopeless to resist.

I begged my colleagues not to discuss that problem. We could not control the national destiny. We must limit ourselves to the pressing duties at Narvik.

Perhaps it would be best to have as many people as possible evacuate. In any case, the city authorities would have to take over the food administration. Many things might still happen.

Not much was said. Some further bits of information were reported. Mr. Toft, who recently had been made head of the Ofoten Railway, announced that they had managed to send out an extra train after the

FROM THE PRIME MINISTER OF NORWAY'S INTRODUCTION

"For another six years he helped his fellow citizens to govern themselves by our well-tried methods of free discussion and co-operative endeavour, and then the wide world suddenly struck Narvik with that shattering impact which woke us all from our long dream of peace."

early morning express had left for Sweden. It had been packed with hundreds of civilians who lived in the vicinity of the railway, but it had been stopped at Hundalen Station, since the Nordal viaduct was out of order. All evacuees would have to go by sea routes.

We decided upon an evacuation of as many civilians as possible. To avoid the risk of an unplanned flight Director Hoel of the Iron Company, the Chief of Police, and I were asked to prepare an appeal to the citizens. The city would also gather complete information on the food stores left in town. Hoarding must be prevented.

Later the same day, I was given an opportunity to make a statement over the local radio station. I explained that the railway was not operating, but that boats might be used. Everyone must remain as calm as possible and not take too much luggage along. I wanted to add more but was cut off by the German censor.

Between one and two thousand citizens left town the first day, but it was impossible to carry out any detailed plan. There was no panic, but people left in complete uncertainty. We had no information as to what localities the Germans might declare forbidden zones. We feared for the northern district, since two German destroyers had gone in that direction at early dawn.

North of the city are two fjord arms. The ocean goes in to Rombakken in a long thin arm where the mountains stand almost vertically above unpopulated fjord shores. To the west of the Øyjord peninsula the Herjangen fjord opens to a broad bosom. The inner fjord has forests and open fields. Here Bjerkvik lies, a friendly little village with a church and a large new school building. Three or four miles up in the valley lies Elvegårdsmoen, the military training camp. Hundreds of families left for Øyjordtangen. We received news that the summer cottages there were crowded and that transport difficulties beyond that point were great. German troops were marching north. We got a telephone call through to Bjerkvik but the youthful telephone operator was confounded and did not know what to say.

The City Council room became a kind of headquarters. We sat at the long table and received reports.

The boats with evacuees had not returned. That was the first sign. There were free districts where our people began to make free decisions.

Oslo Radio announced that Quisling had been made Prime Minister, that all was quiet, and that we must co-operate with the Germans. The King and the Government had fled.

A round little woman came rolling in, completely out of breath.

The German soldiers were buying up all the chocolate in her store and they paid only in funny little paper money. What was she to do?

F

There was nothing to do about it. But she might conceal the best chocolate. Sell candy in small bags.

Yes, but the money?

That's German money which the banks are compelled to exchange.

The Head Surgeon on the phone: "Where shall we bury our dead?"

The merchants called. They could not ration food without regulations and cards. There must be law and rules. They had old customers who wished to buy.

Calm down. Sell as little as possible. We will print cards.

And the bakers called.

The Germans are devouring all the pastry.

Let them eat. But don't bake any more.

Did the Mayor know where to get a pair of trousers for a navy cook who had been blown ashore in his underwear?

Odd calls.

"This is the Commerce Bank calling. Does the City not need more cash?"

"Yes, but wasn't a man from the City Treasurer's Office just in to get money?"

"True enough, but don't you want more? The money is being exchanged pretty fast."

"Of course. Thank you for calling. We will send for more immediately."

The citizens had heard they should not believe Oslo Radio. The Germans had taken over the station.

"Tromsö Station says we are at war."

The messenger boy we had sent to Øyjord returned.

"I took a rowing boat across," he reported. "The Germans had taken the ferry. People out there don't know what to do. The highway to the north is closed. The military camp at Elvegård is taken."

The man with the radio news came back.

"I got Stockholm. They announce that all leading harbour cities in Norway have been conquered and that there is confusion throughout the country. But Tromsö says that there was an all-night battle in Oslofjord and that the Capital was conquered from the air. Also that the King and the Government escaped and have ordered general mobilization."

What shall we do with Øyjord?

Widow Johansen on Street 2 refuses to ration.

Evacuees are fleeing along the railway tracks, but we have heard shooting from that direction. Shall we try to stop them?

Karlsen is drunk again and fought with a German soldier. They dragged him away. There are other drunks, too.

The Hospital has issued an emergency call for trucks. The cellar is full of corpses. But Commander Askim is pulling through.

The Germans have taken all trucks.

For a while it appeared to be almost hopeless to try to put order into the chaos the men of the New Order had created. Then a few of us moved to an inner private office. We posted a sentinel at the door. All the errand boys in town were used as special official messengers. Our orders were in writing and signed.

The Liquor Store must be closed.

Disloyal merchants will have their stores confiscated.

Placards were posted announcing that advice on evacuation could be had at the City Hall. Admittedly we had no other advice to give than to take things calmly till we could get more information.

People were sent to Øyjord carrying written powers of attorney.

The northern territory was banned, including both the railway to Sweden and the highway to Bjerkvik.

Calm down.

The day was a nightmare of activity and we thanked God for that.

How could it have happened? There was no time to contemplate and consider.

Norway was at war. In northern Norway a gun had never been fired at a human target. But we were about to learn the lesson of war to the last bitter detail.

The British Come

WE slept like logs that night and were still dazed when we were awakened by the first gun shots the next morning. They came at the same hour as on the day before with the same heavy detonations. Again we heard Siri's tripping feet, this time before we were out of bed.

"Isn't it Christmas to-day either?"

"No, it is war."

"Is war nice?"

No, war was not nice, but it was undeniably exciting.

When we drew the curtains from the windows we saw fiery tongues all over the harbour. The clouds hung low but the fog was not quite as thick as on the previous day. Thunder came from the fjord and the harbour replied.

"Who is firing out there now?"

"I don't know. Whoever it is, they are friends, and their aim is excellent."

We saw direct hits on several of the ships in the harbour. The flames were so intense that the metal itself seemed to be burning.

Shells rained upon the harbour and debris from the mail pier sailed through the air and whistled above our home. For a time we had to flee into the basement. It was a bit cold down there and we were in night clothes. I ran upstairs for some heavier clothing, but was fascinated by the sight from the windows. One of the German destroyers was afire from stem to stern. Its engines were still operating but it circled aimlessly without direction or plan.

From the basement, "Aren't you coming back? Siri is cold."

"I must see this. Our protectors are burning in the harbour."

"They won't stop burning if you bring our clothes."

But, after I had delivered the clothes and returned upstairs, there was nothing to be seen but smoky fog. The cannonading was withdrawing to the outer fjord. It lasted for hours. Even in the late morning, after we had started office work again in the City Hall, we could hear violent explosions from the outer fjord. But this time we knew what was happening.

The first of the wounded had told the story at the Hospital. British destroyers had entered the harbour opening before the Germans had discovered them. This time the British had let go first. The leader of the German destroyers was blown up and a Commodore Bonte had been killed. Wounded Germans had talked of his loss as a terrible catastrophe, revealing that Mr. Bonte must have been of considerable importance.

This welcome news, however, did not greatly change the situation in the town. The people insisted on leaving. Most of the rowing-boats disappeared during the morning. Families in sports dress and with knapsacks could be seen everywhere going toward the water front and to the north of the town. We were somewhat worried about this impromptu evacuation.

It might prove difficult for small boats to get through to the unoccupied territories. Now even the south side, called Ankenesstrand, had been taken over by the Germans, who had also confiscated the ferries.

We had to try to put the brakes on the evacuation. Panic must be prevented. We at the City Hall told the people that we had wives and children ourselves and that they would be among the last to go.

At the City Hall things began to move in a fairly orderly fashion. The Rationing Board worked under heavy pressure. Ration cards had been printed and the amounts fixed. The system was so devised that any further reductions which might become necessary could be effected without printing new cards. We had enough flour and canned goods. There were huge stores of fish waiting to be exported to Germany. Now the customers had put in a personal appearance. We lacked ice, however, and had to salt the fish. The result was not all that could be desired, even though the fish did taste better than it smelled. We were all to have salt fish for dinner every day during the two months of war to come.

Many committees were organized. A widow enlisted the aid of a group of young girls and organized a soup kitchen. Anyone could eat there if he showed a reasonable need and secured a ticket book at the City Hall. Money was no issue, but there must be order.

From the Hospital came an emergency call for extra help and trucks. The dead were now lying up the cellar stairs.

"We haven't sufficient trucks."

"Make the Germans haul them away."

"They are their corpses anyway. Incidentally, we now know who Commodore Bonte was. The German surgeons here say he was their Supreme Naval Commander. He and his whole staff were blown to kingdom come this morning. They had ten destroyers when they arrived yesterday. Looks as though half of them are more or less destroyed already."

"Excellent. We will confer with the Germans about the dead ones."

Our own Red Cross had more than enough with its own. A complete reorganization had been necessary. The excellent ladies who had sewed and knitted and drunk coffee for the benefit of the cause through the years were of little help now. We needed young boys who would always be ready to go to work. The ladies shown on the Red Cross posters in white aprons, with little morphine syringes, would do no longer. Instead, we needed young fellows who were willing to go out when shots were fired and who knew how to use shovels and tarpaulins.

The new Red Cross Corps was organized into emergency patrols and a First Aid Station was equipped in an auditorium in the City Hall. Arne and Finn, two boys just out of trade school, became patrol leaders, and Deacon Njöten, the church sexton, supervised the First Aid Station. He was a quiet little man with a half-moon, reddish, innocent face. He had married a mighty and broad-bosomed school teacher and had never made any attempt to set the world on fire, but he was going to prove himself one of the most valuable men in the town during the weeks to come.

Germans called frequently at the City Hall. They wanted the keys to the Prayer House, the Public Schools, and other institutions which they had requisitioned for quarters and military hospitals. They did not like to break into these buildings, they said.

We called upon the teachers in the high schools to serve as interpreters and we tried to get as much as possible in writing. It perhaps made little difference just how the Germans stole our property, but we felt that we should have some kind of form for the transactions. Also we had to prevent panic, and we thought that the use of written documents might help bolster our self-respect in the face of the German lawlessness.

We knew that the Germans preferred to act through the Norwegian authorities. But, if they imagined that they could make us appear to be sharing their responsibility, they were badly mistaken. We made it a point to see that our citizens fully understood the true situation. Now we benefited to the full from the open-door politics of a free people. We had no leaders but those who had been entrusted with power by the people.

The Germans had already posted placards in Norwegian text. The sentence construction was somewhat awkward and strange, but the contents were clear enough. The German *Wehrmacht* had come to protect us and would defend our land and people against all attacks, while we on our side would be shot as traitors if we attempted to do the same thing.

As things developed the German *Wehrmacht* did not have much time to spend on us the first few days.

"The first British attack has been victoriously repulsed, but it is not beyond the cowardly British to return," a strutting little German orderly confided to us. He was kept constantly running back and forth between the two hotels and the City Hall with requisitions and announcements. We called him *Sauerkraut*. We understood that the Germans were waiting for "the cowardly British." They kept up an incessant transport of heavy logs and rails out to Framnes peninsula and to the shores beyond.

At Kittenshill the neighbourhood became so unattractive that we loaded bedding and jam jars on a sled and moved downtown. Siri thought it great fun to go on a picnic so early in the spring. But, when we told her that it might be some time before we could return, she insisted on taking old Trine along. She wanted to bring all the toy animals from under the bed but finally limited herself to the Polar bear called Truls. It would be too cold for the rest of the zoo.

From then on we stayed in three different places as the city was gradually evacuated, district by district. Most of the time we slept on the floor in the sitting-room in a teacher's house. We did not think it wise to sleep on the second floor in case there should be more shooting from the sea. The teacher and his wife slept in the dining-room.

The day we moved into town an old railway employee came to visit me. He was secretive and we went into a room where we could be alone. He told me that his telephone line did not pass through the Telephone Building, where the Germans had a twenty-four-hour tapping service. He had access to a direct railway telephone line which reached to the first station on the other side of the Swedish border. We went to his home and made immediate connection with the border village of Riksgrensen in Sweden. I got a Swedish officer on the line. We were both highly excited. I gave all the information I had.

No, the Germans had no planes or heavy artillery. They numbered no more than five thousand men.

He promised to try to get the information through to the Norwegian Government. We made a date for a later call, but, alas the Germans had listening posts established throughout the whole line the next day.

Later in the day, we had an air-raid alarm. The new sirens at the Iron Company and the Royal Hotel functioned perfectly, but not many people went into the cellars. It was an Allied air attack. We counted a total of seven planes, two of a peculiar type. Through my open window I heard some of the survivors from the *Norge* discuss their nationality. They decided the five were British and the two of the different type Norwegian. They seemed strangely outmoded.

There was firing from all directions. It was the first time any of us had seen tracer bullets. Between Fagernes Mountain and the Sleeping Queen the whole sky was filled with streaks of illumination. The planes took their time over the harbour. We saw bombs fall, not large but many. They hit the water between the ships. Three or four of the planes disappeared behind the mountains, but the rest turned and swooped low. The fire from the German anti-aircraft guns grew more intense. One of the old-fashioned planes kept swinging madly over one of the ships at anchor, like an angry old bird that refused to give up. Several bombs swirled in the air. The sailor boys outside my window insisted they were cans like those used for meat balls on board their own ship.

"Do you believe that our people are making use of empty cans for home-made bombs?" I asked, as we heard one of the "bombs" land with a terrific noise directly on the deck of one of the ships.

"Good Lord, man, the meat balls must still have been inside," the sailor exclaimed.

Sadly enough, it was not one of the destroyers that was hit, but a Norwegian coast-guard vessel on which the Germans had hoisted the Swastika since they had taken her over. All planes escaped to safety across the mountains. We breathed with relief.

The same day the Tromsö Radio Station broadcast an evacuation appeal to the populace of Narvik. New skirmishes might be expected at any moment, they warned. Now our people demanded that we take immediate action. If they were destined to lose their lives, it should not be by Norwegian meat balls and cooped up in a town with Germans and rotten fish.

There was nothing for it but to try our luck. I brought along the Chief of Police and a high school teacher whose special field was the German language. The others of us knew German, even though we did not speak it to perfection. We got an audience with General Dietl, who introduced us to his Adjutant, *Korvettenkapitän* Reichmann, a stunning, polite man with an iron-hard face. His heels clicked like a pistol shot. We voiced our case and explained that there were still thousands of women and children left in town, that we were facing a shortage of food, and that it could not be in the interest of the Germans to detain them if there was to be more fighting for possession of the city.

"The British have already sustained one defeat. It is not likely they will return for another."

"But our citizens want to leave."

"We won't stand for any panic, gentlemen."

"There is no panic, but the people want to bring their families out into safety."

"They are safe here," The General turned his back.

"But——"

"The General has no more to say. Sorry, gentlemen, the General is exceedingly busy." *Korvettenkapitän* Reichmann politely saw us to the door. He clicked his heels.

On our return from the Royal Hotel we were met by a crowd which had gathered in front of the City Hall. They saw us come and opened a way for us toward the stone balustrade. I turned and faced the questioning eyes and made some sort of a speech.

We had done our utmost. The Germans refused to let anybody evacuate. We had to face things as they came. We must prove ourselves Norwegians and not behave like a flock of frightened chickens. Should there be any food shortage, we would starve together.

Later in the evening I was called back to General Dietl at the Royal Hotel. He occupied the room which Consul Gibbs had lived in only a few days earlier. Captain Reichmann was again present. The General looked up from the maps spread before him.

"You have a nice city here, Mr. Mayor," he said.

"We used to like it," I answered.

"And what magnificent mountains! Beautiful Nature, excellent ski-ing terrain. Better than on the Swedish side. I once spent a holiday at Abisko, only fifteen miles across the border."

"The General wishes to confer with the Mayor about the conditions for the publication of a newspaper," Captain Reichmann interrupted.

"That is correct. I regret that I could not grant your request this morning, but we wish life to continue as normally as possible. Your people must return to work."

"The General means the ore export?"

"Well, that will begin again in good time. But all other work."

"The railway and the ore export are the mainstay of our employment."

"You can fish."

"We have no boats."

"You can fish from the shores."

Herr Reichmann again interrupted.

"Herr General wants to say that all work must be started again insofar as the military operations will permit. This must be announced in a newspaper which you will be permitted to publish. All copy must be approved before you go to press."

"And we must encourage people to fish from the shores?"

"We will return to the details in proper time." The Captain was stiff. The General was lost over his maps.

Captain Reichmann invited me to his private room.

General Dietl looked up.

"We will become friends, Mr. Mayor, later," he said, "when we learn to know each other better."

He spoke as though he were announcing an item fairly far down in the programme, an item that might some day be of interest.

We left. It was the last time I saw him.

Captain Reichmann did his best to be friendly.

"You somehow have not complete confidence in us, have you, Mr. Mayor?" he said.

"We *are* enemies," I answered.

His face turned hard and white.

"Do you still listen to the English?"

"We listen to the Norwegian Government."

"There is no longer a Norwegian Government."

"We think there is."

"Do you think we can become friends on that basis?"

"I never said so."

"Your attitude will be changed. Do not our soldiers behave well?"

"You mean the first morning?"

"You know perfectly well what I mean. Have we looted anything in the town? Don't we pay for all we get?"

"Yes, with occupation currency."

"What's wrong with that, don't your banks have orders to exchange it?"

"And what are the banks going to do with it?"

"That will be taken care of in the final settlement. We will see to it that England pays. They started this war. You shall see that we are one day going to make England pay even you."

"The war is not over yet."

"It won't last many weeks now."

I rose.

"You mentioned we could publish a newspaper. What are the conditions?"

"No conditions, but we must see all copy."

"I will confer with our newspaper men and you will hear from us to-morrow."

The following day we had our manuscript finished. Part of it consisted of rules for rationing and part of it of appeals for unified sacrifice and co-operation, all held in a fairly general tone. We had attempted to use words with a double meaning, and hidden appeals were made in some places. Alas, most of the first ones were discovered and deleted. The Germans had good interpreters. I met two of them, Corporal Wiedener, who spoke excellent Danish, and a private who spoke Norwegian with an East Norwegian accent. The private was exceptionally slimy. It seemed to be of the utmost importance to him to show his friendliness. We did not return it. He had evidently received his share of Norwegian kindness already. From his accent we knew quite accurately where in our land he had been enjoying Norwegian hospitality as a "Vienna-child" after the last war.

The newspaper which finally resulted did not make too good reading, but it might perhaps do some good. It did not carry much news; but, on the other hand, it was not humiliating. It had a Norwegian profile and it was going to be the last Norwegian newspaper printed in Narvik.

But the citizens received accurate news as well. At the moment when Captain Reichmann was busying himself at the Grand Hotel with proof-reading, typewritten radio news bulletins were circulating all over town. Fat little Instructor Tanke was the editor and publisher. His work was surrounded with the utmost secrecy and was painstakingly correct.

Now, at long last, we began to get a full and correct picture of what had happened on the war front in southern Norway. The Germans had already been made to pay severely. The first day a number of German warships had been sunk, among them the cruiser *Blücher* with the entire Gestapo force destined for the Norwegian scene. Thousands of corpses had been floating in Oslofjord.

Long after the fighting had begun the German ultimatum had been presented to the Norwegian Government.

We must place our entire coast line at the disposal of Germany. We must surrender our airfields and our communications. The fortifications must be delivered intact. We must give up our merchant fleet and break all contact with the Western Powers as well as with the American continent.

Together with this ultimatum the German Minister had delivered a personal message from Hitler to our King, "whom he highly respected." He wished the Norwegian King would appoint a more "co-operative" cabinet under the leadership of Major Quisling.

We heard that none of these demands had been given a moment's consideration. We heard of the courageous stand taken by the King and the Government and how the Norwegian Storting had met in the midst of the violent war zones and had authorized the King to continue the war, how other German diplomats in Oslo, at a moment. when the diplomatic conferences were still in session, had led advance attack patrols north along the highways with the intent of taking the King and the Government prisoners, and how the new Commander-in-Chief, General Ruge, with a band of fresh minutemen, had stopped them a few miles south of Elverum. His men were in the main farmers and lumberjacks who had volunteered the moment they heard of the German sneak attack.

We heard how Hitler had followed up his "respect" message to our King by having his bombers hunt him from place to place through Trysil before the Norwegian mobilization had become effective.

We could now follow the progress of the war. Front upon front became established. After three days there were six front lines. The King and the Government were still in mortal danger. Our boys fought in the forests, they fought in the mountains, they were giving their lives for the hard, beautiful land which we called ours. But they made the Germans pay dearly.

I can still see the faces of our young boys when they came stealing up the back stairs in the City Hall to read the news bulletins. They did not say very much. Their faces were emotionless, but their eyes spoke. They were like a scream or a prayer: *Weapons!*

Thunder in the Fjord

WE did not hear much about our own front up here. The naval battle of April 10th was already an old story. Via Swedish radio we heard that three of the British destroyers had been sunk, *Hardy*, *Hunter*, and *Hotspur*, but that two remaining had escaped. There were thus five Britishers to the ten in the German flotilla, and almost half of the latter had been put out of action. The German victory did not seem too overwhelming.

But the radio did not mention the fighting in the mountains near the Swedish border at Björnefjell. A skier had brought in news about the fighting in that sector. It was evident that our local boys had not yet been able to establish contact with the other Norwegian forces. We were the forgotten war front.

The same evening German Headquarters asked for a copy of the City Roster. The protectors wanted a complete list of their protégés.

The following morning, Saturday, the 13th of April, came the first week-end of the war. It was destined to become Our Day. Our front sector was, after all, not forgotten or neglected. In the morning we heard the King broadcast a strong personal appeal to all Norwegians. He could not reveal where he was, but he was with the Crown Prince and the Government. They had all escaped a murderous bombing attack. He had seen defenceless cities bombed by the Germans. He encouraged his people to continue resistance and to fight.

Early in the afternoon we heard heavy gunfire again from the outer fjord, increasing in violence. The German-occupied sectors of the town were evacuated and the Alpines marched out towards the north side. Troops were left behind to defend the harbour and to hold the Telegraph Office.

A young fellow came running from the direction of Framnes. It was my friend Oscar.

The Germans had chased him away from the sea view, but he had seen the whole fjord swarming with ships. The whole British fleet must be there. Among them was a colossus of a warship.

I thanked him. "Now we are getting some real benefit from your curiosity." I said. "Call again."

No German orderlies with requisitions appeared on that day. It was hard to buckle down to work. We were tense and watchful. We could not see much of what was taking place in the fjord, but we did hear that the centre of the fighting was moving closer. Some shells flew in over the harbour, and several struck in the city proper. We stood at the windows. We ran through the streets. We hid behind the corners when we heard the shell splinters whine through the air. Women and children were placed in the comparative safety of the cellars and basements. A subway was under construction beneath the Iron Ore Company. It was only partly completed and the raw-cut cliff walls lacked their concrete finish. Water was continuously streaming down the walls, and the floor was only loose planks. But it was said to be bombproof, and, it could accommodate one thousand people. That day it became very popular.

There was also an excellent basement underneath the Fire Station behind the City Hall. A double shift was kept working there, day and night. We dug two cellars, one under the other. They were strengthened by pillars and equipped with lights and benches.

For those of us, however, who had any kind of excuse for staying up in the daylight world it was impossible to remain quiet. We were burning with impatience. Our destiny was being decided in the fjord. The shooting seemed never to come to an end. Oftentimes the blasts made one continuous sound effect. Then quiet reigned again. We could distinguish the heavy shots; these must come from the largest guns. The mountains hurled the sound like a ball back and forth among themselves. Once we counted the echoes up to seven.

We felt like the princess in the fairy tale about whom the princes were fighting. We felt the joy and the pride when the white prince rode in with victory and also the humility of being only a passive prize. The horrifying inactivity of it all!

We heard a deafening explosion from the harbour, even though the thunderous cannonading itself was drawing northward. The deserted streets were again filled with people. We saw German soldiers come from Framnes forest on the opposite side of Hospital Hill. They were wet and weak. Many had thrown away their weapons. And we acknowledged for the first time a strange peculiarity of the human mind, a psychological reaction which many of us were to be given a chance to experience. After mortal danger the reaction takes the form of a psychic intoxication. Now we witnessed how the stone-like stares of the stiff German sailors were transformed into half-delirious laughter and smiles. Many of them went through the streets, arm in arm, singing. They stopped to chat with us. We were told that it was a British battleship which was out there on the warpath together with other British craft. The German squadron was at this moment engaged in a death struggle inside the narrow Rombaksfjord to the north.

When we told them that their number was up, they only smiled forlorn smiles and muttered "*Kamerad.*" They were certainly no longer the *blitz* men. They looked rather like half-drowned cats nestling close to one another in order to keep warm. Nor were they any longer condescending in their attitude towards their "racial brethren" who had been so tragically led astray by the decadent democracies. Now they wished to be accepted because they were human beings like us and because it was good to be alive. They had lost their contact with their officers and their morale was gone.

Bands of beaten Germans continued to drift through the town and up Fagernes Mountain. Laboriously they trampled a path for themselves, zigzagging their way up the steep slope. Their dark rows stood against the snow wall like curving snakes.

An old woman came down the hill with her mattress on a sled. She owned a little cabin up on the ridge, but now it was packed with Germans. She told us that they had asked about the way to Sweden and that she had pointed skywards. They could march endlessly in the mountains before they discovered that there was no way leading through.

There was not much life in our streets any more. It was limited mainly to the German sentinels and an occasional truck with corpses under tarpaulins. The dead came from the sea. Our own Red Cross patrols were kept busy. There were as yet not many wounded among the civilians. In emergencies our Red Cross workers gave a hand to the enemy.

Even though I belonged only to the Red Cross reserve I felt an urge to see things for myself. In any case, observation might offer some relief from the nerve-wracking impatience which burned us all. I put the Red Cross band on my arm and went to the piers. Perhaps there might still be some wounded there. At intervals shells still burst in that vicinity.

In the street above the pier I found the doors of the Seamen's Home standing open. All the rooms were filled with bedding and German uniforms and articles. On the tables were the remains of meals, but there was not a living being in the entire building. It had been used as a barracks by the invaders, and they must have left in great haste. On the shelf above one of the beds lay a diary and a pile of snapshots. I put them in my pocket and left the building.

The harbour itself was a ship graveyard with wreckage wherever one looked. Flocks of frightened sea gulls screamed in the air. Occasionally they dived hurriedly into the waters to nip at some of the strange objects that floated in the oily sea. The pier itself was a tragic sight. The new cold storage vault that we had built was gone except for some falling brick walls. The installation of the heavy machinery had never been completed. We had planned the dedication for the last days of April. The creamery on the other side of the square had also been hit. One wall had a gaping hole and all the windows were blown out, but the building itself might perhaps be repaired. The piers looked hopeless. The wooden planks of the old pier had been blasted away. The wooden pillars projected from the water like so many stumped teeth. The new pier was torn apart. The huge concrete block at the end had been cut in two as by a huge axe. Everywhere were strewn bits of wreckage. Parts from ships were thrown ashore among timber, logs, and cleft rocks. Whole parts of warships lay in silent testimony to the terrific force of naval artillery fire.

It was the strangest sight I had ever witnessed. I felt as though I were walking around the playground of a huge monster who had suddenly tired of his toys. The whole inside of a warship seemed strewn around. It was like a gigantic jigsaw puzzle which had been left unfinished. One could, however, somehow guess that, if the parts were brought logically together again, they would make up a warship or, more accurately, one of those German destroyers which had brought to Narvik the chaos of the New Order. How these pieces had been clipped off and thrown around between our piers was a riddle that baffled me.

But we had long since stopped our wondering. Life had become very strange during these latter days. I knew, however, that I should have been greatly surprised, if someone at that moment had told me that I was going to have the riddle solved a year and a half later, in the peaceful little town of Beloit, Wisconsin, and that I would find it in a book written by a German officer who even at that moment was watching my aimless wanderings along the destroyed pier. And yet it was thus that I got the explanation. One of the ten destroyer commanders, *Korvettenkapitän* Fritz Otto Busch was going to write a thick volume full of Nazi romanticism about the exploit: *Narvik—vom Heldenkampf deutscher Zerstörer*. And he was to send a copy to relatives in the United States from whom a Norwegian-American friend had borrowed it.

The solution itself was fantastic enough. It really was true that the broken mosaic by the pier that afternoon was made up of parts from one of the ten destroyers. She had been the last in line of the German squadron, and they themselves had called her "The Tactical No. 10." She had been mortally wounded in the harbour battle of April 10th and had not been able to participate in the death struggle this fateful Saturday. When the naval battle began in the outer fjord she had been left deserted and tied to the pier. All things removable had been brought ashore and her crew and officers had taken up their position in the railway tunnel above the pier. The destroyer had been changed into a huge floating mine loaded with depth charges ready to explode.

From the observation point up in the tunnel the Germans had followed the battle outside. They saw a British destroyer enter the harbour. She had obviously been hit during the battle and proceeded at slow speed, listing badly. Cautiously the crew manœuvred her between the wrecked ships till they could beach her in shallow water at Ankenes, to the south of the harbour, in full view of the town. The sea bottom was even there and it was low tide.

Then a second British destroyer entered the harbour. She was in battle trim and looked as though she were hunting more opponents. When she discovered the silent German destroyer along the pier she approached cautiously. A dynamite expert stole down from the tunnel. He started the timing device and escaped to safety. The mine was set for ten minutes. The British destroyer continued its approach. The distance to "The Tactical No. 10" was now only about two hundred yards and grew constantly less. Suddenly a shot burst from a German machine-gun nest planted among the wooden pillars beneath one of the iron-ore piers. The soldiers there had not been informed. The British changed their course and were out of danger when the German ship exploded.

It was this terrifying explosion that we had heard earlier in the afternoon. As I stood on the shell-torn pier and prayed for telepathic powers to call our allies to land I did not know that one of their ships had already been there, that she had barely escaped a death trap, and that she had left again since she did not carry invasion troops.

I kept watch on the beached British destroyer across the harbour, not more than a mile or so away. She was not so badly damaged that she could not fire and she kept sending shells against the German machine-gun nest beneath the ore pier. I could see the propellers whip the water and I hoped each moment that she might get off again.

I might be running the risk of having the people over there take me for a German, so I kept the arm band with the cross turned towards the sea.

At last I tired of standing at the pier and turned to walk towards the shell-torn warehouses. Turning a corner, I ran into a German lieutenant. He had a revolver in his hand. His face was tense, his jaw jutted forward.

G

"I had you at dead aim all the time," he said. "If you had attempted to contact the gentlemen across the water, you would have been a dead man. I can assure you of one thing, and that is that your friends the British will never come!"

I shrugged my shoulders and went into the town. I met one of our Red Cross cars in Street 1. It was packed with boys of the Fire Brigade, most of whom also functioned as Red Cross helpers. The car they were using had been put at their disposal by the Iron Ore Director. It had been an elegant old automobile, with tasselled curtains at the windows; but, since it had been given hard usage by our Red Cross after the war began, it was pretty badly battered. We drove around the town for a while. The city itself was deadly quiet. The guns' thunder from the fjord had stopped. Off and on an explosion came from the direction of Rombaksfjord.

As we drove past the Market Place we saw the swastika still flying from the Telegraph Building. An idea struck me. The German service chief was still on duty, compelling Norwegian operators to make telegraph and telephone connections.

It might prove helpful if it did not function too well at this particular time. This was the only central office and so far as we had been able to learn all the German communication lines passed through it. It might at least do no harm to create a little extra confusion. Something must develop very shortly. The way had been blasted open for our allies.

We stopped and entered. Corporal Wiedener received us with a smile and his best Danish. He was obviously nervous. I made my face as sombre as a swastika and assured him that the game was up. The city was once more Norwegian. We were expecting the British in town at any moment. They were already disembarking.

He was not feeling too good.

I continued:

The German troops had fled the town. He could see for himself through the windows that not a dog was left in the streets.

The Corporal in his shocked fear dropped into the German: "Ach, but I am not a combatant, I am a telephone watchman."

"But you carry weapons."

He delivered his pistol, clicked his heels, and declared himself to be my personal prisoner.

I clicked my own heels a little to make it official. But I am afraid I scratched my head in a rather unmilitary fashion. What was I going to do with the poor devil? When I just asked him to disappear, the Corporal regained his dignity to a considerable extent and asked for a receipt for his pistol.

I became brusque once more, and tried to look as mad as a colonel at morning parade.

What? Did he not know the simplest war rules? Baggage receipts are not issued in such instances!

He left.

But I had to disappoint the Norwegian telephone operators by telling them that I had not told the gospel truth. Our troops were not yet in town. It was high time we were all off. The Germans might wish to continue the use of the station until the last minute and it would be best if there were no one to assist them.

"But there are more sentinels in the basement!"

"Oh! That's bad!" I said. Perhaps I had let myself in for something.

But even they let themselves be bluffed. They refused, however, to give up their weapons.

Well, they could take their weapons along and march off.

And off they went. We saw them march up towards the mountain. They had not gone far, however, before they met another group descending. They stopped. Then they all came storming back towards the Telegraph Building. We jumped into the car and drove off. They fired at us. The right window was smashed, but we escaped. The dignified old car cut the corners so fast that the curtains flew.

At the City Hall we waited deep into the night for the counter invasion. Reports kept coming in, but the invasion did not materialize. The electric lights went out. The power station in Rombakken had evidently been hit. We lit candles and continued with our work.

Two boys had watched the last phase of the battle in Rombaksfjord and brought in a report.

Four German destroyers had been driven in there. One of them had laid itself crosswise, thus blocking the whole fjord, while the three had gone in to the foot where they had beached the ships and saved the crews.

The blocking destroyer had fought to the end. She was laid in a narrow passage and the British were prevented from getting by as only one boat could pass through. The huge battleship that we had seen in the fjord had obviously been unable to get at them. Only the smaller British craft could get within shooting range. The first one which had attempted to force passage had her whole front shot off, but had continued to fight further inside the fjord. Then several British had forced the blockade, and the Germans had been blasted beautifully by the British broadsides. Finally, the last German had been beached, whereupon the Germans blew up all their own ships.

"That was four. But they were ten when they arrived. Let's do some arithmetic."

"Two were sunk in the harbour on April 10th, during the first Britisl attack, and several were hit. One of them capsized at the pier the nex morning. That was the ship of big boss Bonte himself! That makes three in the first battle. And to-day's harvest was four in Rombakken and another sank outside Framnes," said the boy from Beidsfjord. "And we saw one go into Herjangen that went smack bang ashore on the rocks and blew to bits."

"That makes it minus six to-day."

And I myself had seen the remains of one of the destroyers down on the piers this afternoon.

"That's minus seven to-day and minus three before. That makes a perfect score!"

We sang *Tipperary*. That was the only English song we knew by heart except for *My Wild Irish Rose*, which did not seem to fit the occasion. We felt an urge to voice our enthusiasm for the British.

What was going to happen next? We discussed all the possibilities. At intervals we went out into the street to take a look towards the fjord. The sky was grey and we could not discover anything.

A fireman and I walked to the Royal Hotel from where we could see over into Herjangen. We thought we could see a smoke column on the far side of the fjord. That was all. But the hotel was not deserted as yet. The lobby was full of soldiers. They saw us also. Suddenly we seemed to be surrounded by a whole battalion. One of the men shouted that he was sure this was the fellow who had made Wiedener give up his weapons.

Then gun barrels prodded our backs and we were ordered to turn about. First we were going to be confronted with the Corporal at the Telegraph Office.

Yes, I was that fellow!

My companion explained that he had been on duty at the Fire Station all the afternoon.

"There were some men with firemen's helmets, but this one was not among them," the Corporal explained with generosity, and they let my companion go.

I asked him to phone home and tell them that I would perhaps be detained at my office for the night with the Rationing Board.

When my identity had been established I was marched with a guard to Captain Müller. I kept a reasonable and even pace with the gun barrels. By way of consolation I was informed that Captain Müller was the Chief of Espionage and Military Intelligence. He stayed at the Royal.

The Captain was sleepy and angry, but he placed me under arrest in the most correct form, and I was locked up in one of the rooms on the top floor of the hotel. The door was not locked but a sentry was stationed outside.

Section Thirty-Six

FOR the first time I spent a night in the Royal Hotel, which, in a measure, I had been instrumental in getting built. The room was delightful, and it was in no way the fault of the bed that I was unable to sleep.

I had hung my jacket over a chair. Some papers peeped out of one of the pockets, the book and photos I had found in the abandoned German quarters at the Seamen's Home. Even at 2 a.m. there was enough light for reading. The snapshots were of Norwegian soldiers. They must have been taken just before the war. Most likely they had been taken from Norwegian prisoners. But the book was German. It was a diary, half-filled with notes and observations. The German Gothic hand was a little difficult to decipher, but the handwriting was as clear as a pupil's just out of grammar school. DIARY OF KLAUS HERMAN KLAUSHAUSER it read in block letters on the front page. The first entry was dated *April 7, 1940. On the high seas.*

From that night's reading I learned that Klaus was a very young man and that, although he was not afraid to fight against the whole world, he preferred to do his fighting on land. He did not reveal directly that he had been seasick on the way north, but his description of the twelve hundred and fifty mile sea voyage from Bremen to Narvik was limited to brief, staccato sentences telling of roaring waves crashing against the deck and the great congestion aboard the destroyer. In addition to crews of two hundred and fifty there were equal numbers of Alpine troops on each ship. Klaus himself appeared to be an Alpine from Steiermark. He made a comparison between the Norwegian landscape and the mountains of his home valley.

The departure from Bremen was mentioned. There had been neither father nor mother nor girls, promising to send him letters. But there had been a parade on the evening of April the 6th and speeches by the officers. The men had not been told where they were going but they had heard that they were about to have an opportunity to fight for the *Führer* in one of the most daring military expeditions of history.

They had talked among themselves in the hammocks in the narrow corridor of the destroyer about what adventures they were about to experience. Most of them guessed it was to be Scotland. It was not until the 8th of April that they were informed that the expedition was headed for Norway.

"We did not know very much about the country or about the people we were going to visit," Klaus wrote. But a statement about Norway had been posted on the bulletin board, giving a detailed description, so that they might know everything about the Norwegians before their arrival.

"We learned that the people of Norway were honest and Nordic," he wrote, "and that they never locked their homes. They were slow, like our peasants in Friesland, and suspicious towards foreigners. They had lagged behind in modern progress and did not know anything worth mentioning about war. Also, they had been misled by British propaganda. Therefore, the German soldiers must behave as nicely as possible, especially toward women. We were going to take over Norway in order to protect the land and the people.

"That evening we all had beer, and one of our officers saluted the *Führer*, who had entrusted us with this crusade. We were to protect our racial brethren and bring the New Order to the Land of the Midnight Sun. We all held on to our chairs and roared '*Sieg Heil.*' "

Thus he had ended his writing for that evening.

There were a few pages about Narvik, but young Klaushauser had not been greatly impressed. Narvik! Why it was only ocean and mountains and a mad people who did not know what was in their best interest.

I put the photos in my pocket and the diary underneath the mattress and tried to get some sleep. The whole thing was so completely ridiculous. We did not understand war and our homes were always unlocked! That was our guilt!

I felt ill, nauseated. Those heavy boots outside the door somehow trampled on all the things we loved and worked for, on all justice and consideration for others, on all that was noble and beautiful, and on all the dreams of happiness and liberty that we cherished. Could it be that all we had worked for had been only a passing dream, an escape from reality?

I got up and walked slowly about the room. From the window I could see the grey, windswept farms across the fjord. Small, crooked birches stood around the homes. In the shallow soil the trees seemed to have braced themselves against the rocks in order to weather the storms.

No, we could not have done differently. Had we furnished enough weapons all alone, to stop the demoniac machine of Nazi violence from breaking over our homes, there would have been no homes left to defend.

I tried to open the windows to get some fresh air. They were tightly closed and made a noise. The sentry opened the door and asked what was going on. I went back to bed. The German soldier remained standing in the open door leaning on his gun. He could not be twenty yet. I asked him.

Eighteen.

And how long had he been a soldier?

He was a sailor, and his ship had been in the midst of it since last autumn when Poland started the war.

He was eager for conversation. The night had evidently been a little long for him, too.

We talked about everything between heaven and earth. Often his answers were as solemn and memorized as from a confirmant on the church floor. *Der Führer hat es gesagt!* The *Führer* had said so.

His view of the world outside Germany could not possibly have been more distorted had he been given an imaginary picture of men on Mars and told they were his neighbours. As for Norway, he obviously thought it was a kind of half-colonized people exploited by international Jewish capitalism.

I told him a little about our country, our social reforms, and our neutrality policy, and asked him whether he thought these things could come from a half-civilized people?

He somehow withdrew, and answered that he had never had opportunity to get much education. Such questions his officer could answer.

His humbleness was genuine. He seemed to find some kind of satisfaction in a relentless self-immolation. And I caught myself admiring this soldier material. To what could one not drive these young men? I had seen the emigrating lemmings up in the mountains, tiny brown creatures that went in closed ranks led by a blind instinct straight through all dangers across rivers and into the sea. And if the waters were too broad for crossing they all drowned instead of turning back.

Now the brown pest had come in a new form. The little animal might be nice enough as an individual with its smooth, young skin, but the herd as a closed phalanx was quite another matter. One hoped it would not become necessary to kill them all off.

But, after all, this was scarcely the right moment to ponder what was to be done with a beaten Germany. At the moment it was she who stood there with the gun in the open door, all powerful, and I who lay defence-less on the bed. And I certainly did not feel arrogant at this particular hour. Yet it seemed contrary to all natural laws that this ignorant enthusiast, this undeveloped youngster with a gun should have power over me.

At last the chief of Nazi sentries arrived and I was taken downstairs. They gave me something that was said to be coffee, although it did not bear much resemblance to our breakfast drink of the same name. Mrs. Polly's regime in the Royal Hotel was definitely a thing of the past.

Then I was placed in the lobby to wait for the prosecutor. My sentry now spoke to me in completely frank comradeship and showed me a picture of his sweetheart in Germany.

The army lawyer was about my own age. I could see that he was not a man with an officer's training. He took down my explanation. I ad-mitted the facts, but said that I had personally believed that the British were about to land. Corporal Wiedener had dressed up his account and reported my behaviour as being far more threatening than was actually the case. When the evidence had been concluded the report was taken to the General for disposition.

I sat waiting. This part of the lobby was a kind of smoking room with a fireplace. It also served as a passage to the dining-room. A steady stream of officers passed through. I heard them mention the British battleship *Warspite*. This was evidently the big ship we had seen during the naval engagement in the outer fjord. The destroyer beached on the other side, at Ankenes, seemed to be the *Cossack*, so far as they had heard. She had been refloated at early dawn. They were all more or less excited, even though it did appear that the morale had been re-established during the night, since nothing more had happened. They raged over the brutality of the British. Those *Schwein* had been firing at German sailors who were crawling ashore.

They, of course, would have waited until the enemy had finished taking their position—I thought.

When the prosecutor returned he was abrupt and a little nervous. He informed me that the General had found me guilty of violating § 36 of the German Military Law having to do with sabotage of communications. Since I was a colleague I might read the law myself.

Section Thirty-Six was not inviting. It carried the death penalty. There was no alternative.

I looked up. The prosecutor smiled grimly.

"I take it you understand," he said.

I nodded.

And then he departed. I remained sitting in the same position. The room was a little chilly and there was a bad draught from the door. I thought the janitor had not made a very good fire this morning.

My guard peeped over my shoulder at the legal papers on the table. There were tears in his eyes as he turned aside.

Only then did I realize that the situation was serious, even though it all seemed unreal in this well-known setting. The morning sun came through the window, flattering Mrs. Polly's burgundy draperies. The others of us on the building committee had to the last urged a more discreet colour, but she had been firm and had shown us the doorman's uniform, already tailored.

Was this, then, really going to be the last day? I hoped it would be over soon. If I could be spared seeing anybody I could stand it. I must not think of those who were left behind. Now there was not much that I could do for them anyhow.

I don't know how long I sat there. In the late morning the prosecutor reappeared. He informed me that he had again conferred with the General and with some of the officers. Because of a plea from the City Council it had been proposed that I be pardoned and the General had finally given his consent. I must give my word of honour, however, to report to Captain Müller every day at 12 noon and at 6 p.m.

I promised.

When I returned to the City Hall I found the atmosphere gloomy. My colleagues had heard of my arrest and early in the morning had sent an appeal to the General. They stressed the fact that I spoke German and that I was indispensable to the civil administration.

I asked for a copy of the appeal. It might come in handy on some later occasion.

For the remainder of the morning, in spite of its being Sunday, we held an emergency meeting to consider rationing problems. A large part of our stores at the piers had been destroyed during the naval battle of the previous day and we had to tighten the rations. This, however, did not constitute our only problem.

We still tried to operate on a monetary system but were very short of ready money. The money went only one way, from the buying public to the merchants. The latter did not wish to deposit it in the banks which were already bursting with occupation reichsmarks.

We discussed the possibility of printing our own local money. Either we must use the German currency in our own dealings or we must put new paper money on to the market. We invited some bankers in to advise us. We were especially concerned with the ethical side of the problem. Naturally, we wished to see as little as possible of the occupation money in circulation, but the main point at issue was whether or not it should be looked upon as money.

One of our revered city councillors who was in the printing trade said, "These insulting slips of paper are shoved at us on bayonet points. We must refuse to accept them as money. If I didn't have to print them on a Saturday afternoon, they would cost no more than ninepence a pound."

But we could not begin with the question of whether they were real money or worthless paper. We had to consider the social side of the case. The moment such a mark note was forced upon us there had been given from the Norwegian side some service or value in return for it. The question was, then, whether the chance merchant or worker who was left with this mark note must carry the loss alone or whether all should do their part in assuming it.

The question became clearer when we followed the logic of the Germans themselves. During the first week they used nothing but occupation marks. Later they threw bag after bag of the paper marks on the counter in the bank and disappeared with our currency. Since then they had used Norwegian money. Did it make any difference? The fact was that they were stealing from society as such, and that each and every one of us, therefore, must pay. Thus it was in Narvik, and the same thing was probably happening throughout the country. Similar questions probably which the whole world would have to face until these organized gangsters one day were stopped.

I reported an incident to illustrate my point of view. The previous Thursday the Germans had taken a bicycle from one of the messenger boys in the street. They explained that they were going to pay; but, as the boy fought for his bicycle, they gave him a receipt and sent him on his way, telling him to go to the Mayor at the City Hall and ask him to write a bill on the German Occupation Treasury. The boy came to me and we wrote a bill. When we came to the question of value, the boy, naturally enough, begged me to set a high price. I refused to exceed the purchase price.

"Why can't those *Schwein* pay?" he asked.

"It is not the Germans who are paying," I replied. "You know you will get nothing but occupation marks, and what will you do next?"

"I'll go straight to the Bank and change them."

"Exactly. And the Norwegian money in the bank is the savings we all have there."

"Damn it, what a mess things have got into!" he replied.

"You are certainly right about that," I sighed.

But then the problem arose as to what kind of money we were going to use. The city was now the only significant employer that still had work projects under way, with the digging of cellars and graves, repair jobs, and clean-up work. We thought we had sufficient funds, but money rolled out rapidly and very little came in. In a few days the City Treasury would be empty.

The banks reported that the City had large accounts outstanding, but that we would have to accept either occupation money or a cheque.

We returned to first beginnings. It really made little difference what we used; but, since we could no longer have currency with the picture of our own chosen King, we certainly would not use the insulting German paper. We decided to print new money. We split a cheque for one hundred thousand kroner into printed five-krone notes. They became quite popular with the citizens and I do not doubt but that our distressed city did come out a few kroner to the good, since many of these notes were kept as souvenirs and disappeared from circulation.

Having settled this phase of the economic problem, we went on to rationing and employment. Not all things could be rationed. It was to be expected that the initial confidence in the new money would sink and that everybody would attempt to buy something. Stocks were already so limited that difficulties might arise if we did not drastically curtail the buying power. It was still more important to keep alive the strong feeling of our unity in distress. If the liberation of the town were to be long delayed, the good morale we had might be destroyed through an ever-growing impatience with living conditions. It was of paramount importance to keep as many as possible employed. Work gave release and created community spirit.

Accordingly, we put into operation a plan for expanded activity in all fields. Our excellent old City Planning Engineer was appointed chief of the whole public works system. He did not need much sleep and worked, practically speaking, day and night. He worked out plans for the reinforcement of more cellars, the changing of public parks into potato fields, and the laying out of a new cemetery. We decided to take in more workers and more civil service employees, and at the same time expand the activities of the Red Cross and the Fire Department. As a counterbalance, all wages were regulated downward to a minimum, taking into consideration the family burden of each man. As for the people already on the city payroll, they were to be paid only a part of their regular salaries. Everyone was treated alike, not because of any fundamental principle, but simply because we were at war. Even though we had no weapons, we were not going to be deprived of feeling ourselves to be soldiers. We had finally realized that in totalitarian war all the people must do their part and not only the young men with perfect physiques and good teeth.

I received a special salary of ten dollars a week during these months and it was quite sufficient. No one paid any rent. That would have been altogether too complicated as we all were kept moving from place to place. The half-rotten fish was cheap.

Yes, indeed, that Sunday we certainly put through a radical social revolution. Conservative Mr. Toft of the Railway shook his head but admitted that under the circumstances there wasn't much else that we could do. Some days later he instituted the new system among his own employees.

That day, as I returned to our emergency quarters in the Headmaster's house for fish dinner, I was excited and in boundlessly high spirits. I was told that all these rationing nights could not be so dry and boring after all. I said that I had passed a rather interesting night, but that as a gentleman I could not discuss the details.

"Skinny little Mrs. Sivertsen is, after all, the only woman on the Rationing Board, isn't she?" the teacher's wife laughingly inquired.

I knew I was going to sleep like a stone that night. The moment I stretched out on the mattress in the corner it was as though I sank comfortably into a deep well. I saw the surface as a shining halo far above. Bubbles kept ascending. They hung together like section signs.

§ 36, I thought, and was asleep.

XII *Living with the Enemy*

THE following week the General with his staff moved farther inland along the railway line to Sweden. We received news that the Norwegian railway stations in the mountains as well as the private ski huts were being used to quarter German soldiers. The city itself became a kind of outer front sector and we got an *Ortskommandant*, or city commander. I was introduced to the new commanding officer at the Grand Hotel, where he occupied a suite of offices on the first floor. The Grand Hotel was situated a little lower than the Royal and the offices of the commanding officer could not be hit directly by shelling from the sea. The British warships were continuously circling the Narvik peninsula and bombarded the German positions from time to time.

The new chief was Major Haüzel. One glance at him sufficed: he was no good. The type is well known, dominating and brutal, self-satisfied and condescending, with a peculiar, calculating suspicion which covers a secret feeling of inferiority. The type dominates the new Germany. It is the unappreciated geniuses who have taken the power, and the power itself is glorious and mysterious. For lack of a better explanation, it is ascribed to Blood and Race. Not all the German officers are of the Major Haüzel type. If they were, the war could be won more easily.

The majority of them are brilliant technicians trained to severe discipline, and they now follow Hitler as they once followed the Kaiser. In either event, it is a misjudged Germany for which they are fighting, and whether it is called *Grossdeutschland* or *das Herrenvolk* is quite irrelevant. As for the youngsters who have grown to maturity under Goebbels' supervision, the picture is different. They are healthy, well-trained boys who believe in the Blood God, since they know no other.

But Major Haüzel was a man who had followed the new Leader when he was still ridiculous, and such a faith has claim on reward. We guessed that he had been a sour and envious manual-training teacher when Nazism was still confined to the back streets. Now he had come into a dignified position and this dignity the world was going to learn to respect. He had an irritating way of circling a bony, nicotine-stained index finger before one's face when he was giving his orders. He numbered them, *Ein, Zwei, Drei.* He always repeated the last sentence of each section, as if he wished to polish it so that it would stand indelibly in the mind of the mentally inferior listener. I, too, had to count numbers, but silently, in order not to lose my self-control.

When he smiled he was especially obnoxious. He had poor, hungry teeth. He showed them especially in emphasizing that point in the instruction relative to the dull and undeveloped Nordics, for whom, as members of his great race, there was still some hope.

At our first interview, he began with a brief review of the fundamentals of the relationship between the German *Wehrmacht* and the civilians in an occupied country. This philosophic German diatribe was followed by an enumeration of demands which were intended to suffice for the present.

Ein: Quarters must be provided for British sailors taken as prisoners off the ore ships. They need not be too good. The British prisoners had been incarcerated in the Public School, together with the group of Norwegian soldiers given up by Sundlo, but now the Germans needed more room, since the stay was likely to be long.

Zwei: Quarters must be arranged for German sailors of the merchant marine.

Drei: The Major himself needed a new uniform for use in milder weather. Spring would, one hoped, arrive, even in these latitudes.

We explained that there were no more quarters available. All public buildings had already been requisitioned except the City Hall and the Hospital. As for the uniform, we carried none in stock. The Major might try a tailor.

We wished to prevent as long as possible the taking over of private homes, so we found a restaurant in which to house the British prisoners. There was, however, no building that would take care of the German sailors. They numbered about five hundred. Finally, we had to open the beautiful new church in the park at Frydenlund.

We carried on our negotiations through one of the German captains old in the ore trade at Narvik. He deplored the fact that he had received orders to requisition the church. He confided to us that he personally was a religious man, and we made a gentleman's agreement with him. We furnished hay mattresses for his people, and he promised to protect the church property, not to desecrate the altar with guns or foodstuff and to do his best to prevent the installation of anti-aircraft guns in the steeple.

As for the tailor, I committed a tactical blunder. I took him personally to the Major's quarters, to which we were shown by a sentinel. It might be of interest to find out how he had arranged matters for himself.

We were led to a house hidden by a hill down near the Railway Station. The owners had been moved out. The Major took full advantage of the situation to show his patronizing attitude. He kept us waiting for as long a period as fitted his dignity, taking his meal and his after-luncheon rest. The house had been carefully chosen, since it was well protected against fire from the sea. After the audience we were dismissed with a condescending gesture. The samples shown by the tailor were of good English quality, but the uniform was never finished. The tailor constantly found causes for delay.

There would have been no need for our anxiety over being the forgotten front. The British did not stint in their use of ammunition but they did take cautious aim, and, in the beginning, only the German positions were hit.

One night they annihilated a complete German sentry post near Vasvik, the little harbour on the north side of the peninsula with a pier for the ferry and fishing boats. The corpses lay for days before they were buried. The house which the soldiers had been occupying, burned down and not much more than their bones were left. The Germans contended that such remains were not worth burial.

I heard several comments on the British shelling during the two daily visits I was forced to pay to Captain Müller's office.

This was just the beginning. The English were certainly contemplating the utter destruction of the whole city. Only one salvation could be seen —German planes—and they would soon come.

I begged them not to go out of their way on our behalf. The tone of our conversation became progressively more free. To begin with, I thought it was a Gestapo centre; but, when I asked one of the young soldiers, he became so infuriated that I concluded it was a purely military office.

It was well equipped with wireless transmitter, typewriters, and trunks built for index files. The walls were decorated with huge maps of Narvik and the Ofotfjord. They were by far the most detailed maps I had ever seen of Norwegian territory. The text was German. On one general map a heavy black arrow in the fjord bore the legend *Der Weg nach Narvik* —the way to Narvik.

That week we completed our rationing system and put into effect our new wage policies.

The next Sunday morning we had our last contact with Major Haüzel. We were enjoying some tranquil hours in the City Hall bringing the records up to date—all important incidents and decisions were recorded and witnessed—when suddenly Sauerkraut came rattling in. Orders from the Major. He wanted a pair of first-class bedroom slippers delivered at once.

"Slippers, of all things!"

"Soft slippers with stiff toe-caps and low heels."

We patiently explained to him that we did not carry slippers in the City Hall.

"But the Major expressly ordered me to come here to ask for them."

We offered Sauerkraut a cigarette and explained that to-day was Sunday and that it was absolutely impossible on the Sabbath to purchase a pair of slippers in the whole town of Narvik. We finally succeeded in convincing him, and he went on his way.

We had not finished the work with the records before we again heard the tramping of boots in the hallway. This time it was a lieutenant with a whole guard of soldiers.

"*Herr Ortskommandant* wishes, first, to inform you that the ordered articles must be delivered; secondly, that he must have them before 1 p.m. The Mayor knows his address."

The guard clicked all its heels. That was all!

We sat there, not knowing whether to laugh or to cry. They had taken the banks, the schools, and the church. And now slippers on Sunday! It was a humiliating kick in the pants. In this case, counting numbers did not help. We told one another all the jokes we remembered about slippers. It helped a bit. One of the boys had an uncle in the shoe business. He ran out and got a huge pair of slippers that had been used for advertising purposes, and we let the seven-year-old daughter of the janitor deliver them. The child thought it was great fun. She almost had to drag the slippers to the Major's residence.

As we had expected, the Lieutenant soon came rushing back with them. The slippers did not fit. They were too big. He had orders to return them to be exchanged for a pair many sizes smaller. The Major could not understand why such a pair had been sent. We could see, however, that the Lieutenant did.

We were very sorry, but we did not know what size the Major wore. Perhaps the Lieutenant himself would exchange them since he undoubtedly had more knowledge of the Major's feet.

He hesitated a while. He sent the soldiers out into the hallway. We offered him a cigar, and he shrugged his shoulders and decided to go.

It might, after all, save him from another trip. He put the gigantic slippers under his arm and disappeared.

The following day Oscar dropped in again. He had heard of the slipper incident. It was all over town and everyone enjoyed it. Could we make use of him for a trick or two? e had been spying a little on his own and had seen the Germans busy with something down by the shore where it was easy to make a landing. They were burying huge metal containers in the ground. He wished to tell some official about his findings. We went into a secret conference.

Offers to help came in constantly. A middle-aged seamstress offered to make British flags. They might come in handy if there were to be some kind of celebration in town in the near future. It was well that we did not know how long we were going to wait before we could make use of them. Every morning we said to ourselves, "To-day something will happen," but as the days passed we became more patient. "Nothing this week. All right. But next week we shall be free again."

We were without news for several days when the power plant blew up. It took some time to get batteries; the Germans had taken all they could lay their hands on. But Instructor Tanke finally got a fresh supply and the news service again functioned.

We heard that fighting was still going on in all the valleys to the south. British troops had been landed at three points: at Åndalsnes on the west coast; in Namsos, north of Trondheim; and in Harstad, immediately north of Narvik, a little farther out among the islands in the ocean. Later bulletins told that French Alpine troops had also landed. On the southern front and around Namsos our Norwegian troops were fighting side by side with the British within a week after the war had touched Norwegian soil. Farther north it was longer before Allied infantry came in contact with the enemy.

Norwegian soldiers were stationed on the mainland between Tromsö and Narvik. Although the military training camp at Elvegårdsmoen had been occupied the first day, there were Norwegian detachments at many points. The Sixth Division had been mobilized as a border patrol during the first Finnish-Russian war and a major part of it was still under arms. Their Chief, General Fleischer, was a strong and active-minded officer.

For the first three weeks the Norwegians fought alone. The mountains we knew from hunting and fishing trips in summer holidays now became names connected with bloody and bitter battles. The Germans had made good use of their treacherous beginning and had erected machine-gun posts before the Norwegian counter-attack could be got under way. The German soldiers were obviously trained for mountain fighting. They had better weapons, and they fought from well-defended positions. But

H

the Norwegian boys knew their mountains better, and they were their own. We got bulletins of victories, but the advance was slow, and the Norwegian forces did not arrive in time to save the small front sector in the mountains back of the town towards Sweden.

One morning we received a report that Norwegian prisoners were being brought down along the railway tracks. They were the survivors of two hundred Norwegian soldiers who had refused to surrender on the first morning. I knew their commanding officer, Major Omdahl, and was permitted to visit him in the prison. We were forced to carry on our conversation in German, but I did learn that he had managed to contact headquarters on the first day and that Sundlo had disobeyed instructions. The order had been to fight.

Even though we had received no news of Allied infantry activity, the British warships were active. The summer nights were growing steadily brighter and the Germans could never feel secure in their positions. They lay themselves as close as possible to the civilians. They used the little chapel on the outskirts of Northtown for a light artillery position and they installed their quarters and machine-gun nests directly between the homes in the town proper. The exchange of fire grew ever more intense.

One morning Sauerkraut arrived to take me to a new *Ortskommandant*. Now Major Haüzel, too, had moved farther up the railway line. This time the commander was no more than a captain, *Korvettenkapitän* Boehme. But even so the change was for the better. He was more a sailor than a politician, and, also, he was one rank lower than his predecessor, a fact which we construed as a happy omen. The Germans evidently did not wish to be defeated under such a fine creature as a Major. We thought that argument pretty sound, and hoped that the defeat would begin to happen soon. We were growing impatient. Our homes had begun to be somewhat overpopulated. When the Germans, for greater protection, placed their gun positions between private houses, the houses were evacuated.

Captain Boehme gave us permission to visit the English prisoners. Their chief complaints were about the *ersatz* coffee and the "news" that the Germans were giving them.

As for the coffee, I knew about that, but what kind of news was being circulated?

That the Norwegians resented English intervention and that nowhere in Norway was there any fighting going on.

I outlined the true picture of the situation.

As nearly as I could determine I had been talking with Giles Romilly, the nephew of Mr. Churchill. He was in excellent humour but he looked considerably thinner than his famous uncle. I did not see him again. He had been unable to restrain himself, and had rejected with contempt the news reports brought to him by the sentry that evening. The next day I was accused of talking politics with the prisoners, and further visits were denied.

I had looked in vain for Consul Gibbs and his staff among the prisoners. There had been unconfirmed rumours that they had been captured, but no one seemed to know their whereabouts. One chambermaid at the hotel had talked with Mr. Gibbs and his colleagues the morning of the invasion. They had come into the corridor in their robes when the firing began and asked what was going on. She had told them that she had heard in the kitchen that the Norwegian warships were firing on German men-of-war. As far as she could make out the British gentlemen had been busy destroying their secret papers right up to the moment when the Germans arrived. They had just barely escaped. The Royal Hotel was one of the first buildings the Germans occupied. An officer and some soldiers had gone directly to the Consul's room. The maid had been called and they had held a revolver under her nose and one of the soldiers had threatened her in Norwegian. She had replied that she knew nothing, and the Germans seemed too busy with other things to detain her.

We continued to hope that the Consul and his party had escaped and reached Sweden.

On April 21st one of our special messengers reported that the British prisoners had been ordered to prepare to leave. They were under heavy guard, and it appeared that they were to be marched into the mountains. A moment later they came by. I waved to the Captain of the S.S. *Romanby* and he waved back. Among the German guards I recognized the young lover of liberty who had called upon me less than three months before with his plea to be allowed to remain in Norway.

A few days later Norwegian prisoners were also taken away from Narvik along the same railway line on which they had been brought down.

One of the British destroyers accompanied this last prison transport by steaming in close to the shores of southern Rombaksfjord. Shells rained in from the fjord and the prisoners had to run for cover. Two Norwegian officers grasped the opportunity, jumped down the slope and ran at high speed towards the shore, where they were picked up by a boat lowered from the destroyer. We learned, too, that Major Omdahl had also escaped during a snowstorm in the mountains and had reached the Norwegian forces in the North.

That evening we *skaled* for Major Omdahl with German beer. The Fire Brigade celebrated its anniversary in the station cellar. The city had prohibition, it was true; but, since it was only beer and stolen from the German stores, we let the law sleep for one evening. A depot in the harbour had been set on fire by British shells in the morning and the firemen had saved a considerable quantity of flour and had also picked up some of the German stores.

Otherwise, the local prohibition, voted at the beginning of the war, was rigidly enforced. Not a bottle of liquor was sold, even on a doctor's prescription. Only requests from the Hospital were delivered. All the best whisky was sent there as the Germans raised their requisitions, and in inverse proportion to the number of troops stationed in town. At first they had asked for only the best brandy; but, later on, as nothing but younger officers stayed in town, the stars on the bottles also decreased in number.

As the shelling from the fjord grew in intensity the drunkenness among the Germans increased, and we descended still one more grade in the rank of our *Ortskommandant*. The last was a Lieutenant—even though he was *Oberleutnant*—Poetsch. Him we were going to keep.

Poetsch was twenty-nine years old and had been educated as an engineer, but he evidently had been through a more or less continuous military training since boyhood. He used both military and civil titles on his letterheads, requisitions, and military passes. Above all, he was a soldier, and a strutting one, but not without humour. He did not unduly emphasize his dignity as master of the town except when he was issuing disagreeable orders. Generally speaking, he was easy to talk with except when we happened to touch on certain issues. Then it was like clashing with a wall of prejudices that reached to high heaven. There was no shadow of doubt in his mind about the righteousness of the German cause. Might was right, and might meant good guns and well-trained soldiers. After the fall of Belgium and Holland, when the German military machine rolled over France and nothing seemed able to stop it, he walked about in a state of emotional intoxication. Life was wonderful!

The radio bulletins ascribed many of these first victories to Hitler's secret weapons. Under one of the British bombardments we sat side by side in an air raid shelter and I asked him about these secret weapons. If they really were in existence, and were being used they could not be entirely secret. Poetsch laughed.

Selbstverständlich. He would be delighted to entertain me with a military lecture; but, frankly, he had not advanced to a sufficiently high rank to receive such information. But he was not so sure that any new weapons had been put into use, as yet. The ones they had were proving their excellence and they had plenty of them. Oh, if only we could see how hopeless it was to resist! Our people might march with the Germans toward an epoch of world dominion such as history has never seen. Against them we faced only destruction.

"Even if that were true," I said, "we have made our choice. But the war is not over yet. Perhaps it has not even got a good start."

He felt that I was hopeless. In his view I was a fairly agreeable young fellow, a little too old, perhaps, and completely misled by plutocratic propaganda, whatever that may have meant.

He allowed me quite a bit of freedom of action. I even received a personal pass permitting me to be on the streets after eight o'clock in the evening. I had used as an excuse my late evening work in the City Hall, which was true enough. He did not, however, trust me completely. And once or twice he discovered activities of which he disapproved. Fortunately, they were relatively innocent incidents. He learned, among other things, that we had ordered everyone to refrain from speaking to German soldiers except when it was absolutely necessary or when official business was being transacted. But the discovery of this order occurred on a day "filled with unique victories for the German Army," so he overlooked it.

When the *Kommandant* office itself was blown up by British shells, he came to the City Hall every day to issue military passes to Beidsfjord or to the outskirts of town, which had been declared forbidden zones. Some days he brought his "Treasurer" along. Twice a week the plunderings in town were made "legal" through refund payments in occupation currency.

Poetsch was always correct and smiling. Miss Hansen, our not exactly young typist, went so far as to say that this last *Kommandant* really was quite a nice person and that, after all, he probably was only acting under orders.

"Granted that he may be a fairly decent being," one of us coldly replied, "but don't forget that even a tiger has white teeth and isn't the less dangerous for that. Furthermore, it goes far beyond the mere fact of his doing his duty. He is our enemy with all his heart and soul. Each thought he thinks, each breath he breathes, is deadly poison to everything that we call freedom and justice."

"Well, I do not mean that he ought not to be shot even though he is a nice man," Miss Hansen said.

Our friendly relations with *Oberleutnant Diplom-Engineer* Poetsch had, from the very beginning, their clearly-defined limits. On the second day of his regime he found it necessary to exercise his authority. There had been intense firing from the fjord, the night before we received important news from a Beidsfjord peasant who had been wounded by splinters and had come to the Hospital for treatment. He told us that Allied troops had arrived on the other side of the mountains and were quartered in the village of Håkvik.

The same morning Sauerkraut appeared on the scene again. He clicked his heels with extraordinary solemnity. *Herr Ortskommandant* requested the Mayor and the Chief of Police to come at once to his office.

When we arrived we found only the *Oberleutnant* and not much of the *diplom-engineer*.

"Gentlemen," he said, "I have been ordered to inform you that during the night shots were fired in the streets at German soldiers. The perpetrators escaped. They were Norwegian civilians."

"But you took all weapons from us on the day of the invasion," we answered.

"That does not matter. The case is closed."

We thought the Lieutenant was having a joke at our expense. That Norwegians should have hidden weapons and ammunition all this time and then fire a few wild shots in the street and not even hit anyone—there was no logic in that.

The *Kommandant* rose and smiled a hard smile.

"I think the gentlemen do not quite understand the situation," he said, "the case is not open for discussion. I have orders from headquarters to submit a list of hostages who will vouch with their lives for the peace and order of the town. You may name five citizens. I must have their names immediately. Otherwise we must select them ourselves."

The Chief of Police looked to me to give the answer. It was anything but an inviting task.

"You had better begin with us two," I said.

"And three more?"

"Well, we might take the City Engineer, the Head Surgeon at the Hospital, and the Norwegian Manager of the Swedish Iron Ore Company."

They were the best names in town, I thought, four of them at least.

We rose from our chairs, but the *Kommandant* had not finished. "That was *punkt ein. Punkt zwei* is the publication of this news. The gentlemen may personally arrange that matter. You will post public announcements in prominent places in town."

There is that index finger of Haüzel again, I thought. Weren't we through with that devil yet?

We left.

At the City Hall we printed announcements which recorded our conversation as accurately as possible. Perhaps we had emphasized the fact that the supposed firing in the streets had been brought to the *Kommandant's* attention by the German Headquarters in the mountains. But the Germans did not fail to see the irony. Later in the morning, we were ordered to remove the announcements. New placards were posted. The text was written by the *Kommandant* himself.

The same evening the hostages were called to his office and he delivered a speech to us. It came *punkt* by *punkt*. Afterwards, he tried to be friendly and dwelt upon the alibis of the British and the heroism of the Germans. The social atmosphere did not improve. He gave us cigarettes imprinted with gold letters and filled with straw. We were not impressed. The conversation turned to the shelling of the town, which, it appeared, was likely to be worse. We did manage to have some kind of conversation on that subject.

Poetsch asked me to stay after the meeting. He tried to let me know indirectly that he, personally, did not like to use harsh methods, but that he was under orders. He wished to express his personal regrets.

"Completely superfluous," I answered, and offered him a cigarette with tobacco inside. They were no longer to be had in the stores, at least by the new customers.

There were several good reasons why a relatively friendly relation with the *Kommandant* might prove advantageous.

The next day Oscar turned up again at the City Hall. He was bubbling over with excitement. It was almost impossible to prevent him from exploding before we had found a soundproof room in the attic.

He had been asked to convey greetings from a British Admiral, from Poles, and from Frenchmen. Soon there was going to be some real fireworks. Very soon. The Admiral had said so himself. "All right," Oscar had answered. And he had witnessed the execution of a dozen Germans behind a barn. The French had accomplished that. *Fini!*

He was so enthusiastic that he attempted to tell all the stories at the same time.

"Please, please, calm down," I broke in, as I lit a cigarette with deliberate slowness, "and tell me only what you yourself have seen and heard. Only the truth and nothing but the truth, so help you God? You may recall, perhaps . . ."

Oscar smiled. He became a little less tense.

"Well, you remember we agreed that I should go to that lady who was to be my aunt in Beidsfjord. The German pass was all right and I came to her house that same evening. In the night I went on borrowed skis across the mountains to Håkvik. There was only a little snow left in the valley, and I had to leave the skis in the forest. I did not see any soldiers but there were many evacuees from Narvik in Håkvik. There I got a boy to row me out to one of the biggest British warships. I said I had come to report from Narvik and that I had secret instructions from the Mayor and must speak to the Supreme Commander. And I will say that I got to talk with the boss himself. We sat in easy chairs in his cabin and exchanged news over grog and a cigar. I still have my cigar."

Oscar pulled a huge fine cigar from his pocket.

"It had a band on it, but I threw that away so that the Germans would not become suspicious if I happened to be caught. A cigar—why any gentleman must be permitted to carry a cigar."

"But what did you two talk about?"

"Oh, first, I told everything I knew about Narvik and the Germans."

"Wait a minute, how could you understand each other?"

"Well, there was a young officer on board who had some knowledge of Norwegian, and I said 'Sir' and 'All right,' and we understood each other perfectly. I was to convey his greetings."

"Good, but what instructions did you get?"

"First, I was to ask whether you knew anything about the British Consul in Narvik, Mr. Gibbs, and his staff. They cannot have left the town, because they have not sent word out.

"And then he asked me about *morale*. The officer hurried the translation so fast that at first I didn't get that. I thought he meant were the girls here very strict, and maybe I could have given him some information about that, too, but he wanted to know how we felt and on which side we stood. I asked him whether he didn't know that the King had declared war on Germany and that in the whole of Narvik only the nitwit Sundlo did not think that the Germans were so many swine. I told him that we were impatient as hell and eating rotten fish loaded with mustard. Then we shook hands and the Admiral asked me to come again, and I said 'All right, Sir.' "

"But what about those twelve Germans behind the barn?"

"You must be patient. I have just barely finished with the Admiral. As I said, he saw me to the side of the ship and I was put ashore near Sjomen, so I had to walk back to Håkvik. The same day Polish troops and French Alpines, or the Foreign Legion, appeared there. They said that I must not go back over the mountains to Beidsfjord."

"And it was there you learned French?" I asked.

"To be honest, I am no good at French, but they had brought a Norwegian lieutenant along from Harstad, who served as interpreter. I told him what the British Captain had said."

"You told me that he was an Admiral."

"Well, he was Captain of his own ship also, don't you see? Anyway, I was permitted to accompany the French troops in the valley. They marched in single files on the edge of the forest, one on each side of the highway. Turning a curve it happened! You remember that dam at the lower end of the biggest lake? There we were met by a small group of soldiers in Norwegian uniforms. The French had them encircled before they could say 'boo!' I shouted, 'Watch out, they are Norwegians!'

"But at that moment one of them fired his revolver and wounded one of the Frenchmen. The soldier himself dropped in the ditch, with a bullet in his head. The others instantly raised their hands. They spoke in German —one didn't have to be much of a professor to know that.

"The French took all their weapons and marched them a short distance down the road, turning into a farm where an old peasant woman waved as we passed. The prisoners were lined up behind the barn. The French officer asked the Norwegian lieutenant whether he was absolutely certain the uniforms were Norwegian. The Norwegian officer said that he was sure. The Frenchmen took the small metal identification tags which the Germans had around their necks. They turned pale but didn't say anything. The French Officer saluted. One of the Germans took the scarf that he had around his neck and tied it over his eyes. The others did the same. One of them was working frantically at a knot when the shots went off. '*Fini!*' the Frenchman said. That means: 'Now we are through with those swine.' "

"Wasn't it hard to witness all that? You have never seen anyone die before, or have you?"

"I saw them carry home my dad when he drowned in Lofoten, but, of course, that was quite different. Yes, it was a little frightening."

"And how did you get farther?"

"Well, at the upper end of the lake the Frenchmen took up their positions, and I crossed the mountains alone. There were Germans in the woods, but I crept through. At one place I had to lie in a snow cave and act like a block of ice, and I was not far from becoming one. I finally reached Beidsfjord and there I picked up a milk can which I brought into Narvik."

"You have done a nice piece of work, Oscar. It is a pity that I cannot tell the others about it but we had better keep this to ourselves. A man downtown will give you help. You shall meet him to-day. But, when the war is over, we will certainly have a celebration in your honour."

Oscar blushed like a young girl.

"Oh, it's nothing," he said.

We made a date for the next day. I hoped that in the meantime I could get some definite information about Mr. Gibbs. I had a notion where I might search for him.

Some days earlier I had heard two boys talking about a group of unshaved deaf-mutes who were living in a tool-shed not far up in the mountains, no more than half an hour away. They played cards all day long. The Germans had look-outs both above and below. The British were firing intermittently at the enemy positions there, and some civilians had been wounded.

I talked to one of the boys, who gave me a detailed description of these silent men. The descriptions tallied, and I told him who I thought they were. He must help us bring them into town. He was delighted. He had a friend who owned a van that had been used to transport corpses. We might use it.

That evening Consul Gibbs and his colleagues came into town under tarpaulins. We had a house ready for them. We had taken the home of the City Judge, since his family had left town on the morning of the invasion. We had hired both a cook and a maid. Clothes and whisky awaited them on their arrival. As Consul, Mr. Gibbs enjoyed extra territorial privileges as far as liquor was concerned.

The car arrived with the honoured guests: Consul Gibbs, Captain H.W. Torrance, Mr. E. Pegott, and a Commander whose name I never learned to pronounce correctly. They had lived in the tool shed for three weeks, surviving on canned foods. Captain Torrance knew Norwegian, but the others pretended to be deaf-mutes when people happened by. After the naval battle of April 13th the cabin had been packed with German sailors who raged and cursed at the British; and Consul Gibbs, shaking his head and smiling, had poured coffee for the uninvited guests. Typically good-natured and dumb Norwegians, the Germans must have thought. They had, however, enjoyed the coffee.

How the British officials had been able to continue the comedy for so long was beyond my imagination. Even minus their collars and with rough beards, the consular personnel looked typically English. It is not easy to disguise gentlemen, but hot baths, shaves, and fresh clothes did make some difference.

We *skåled*, and I told them that the town counted it a great honour to have them as its guests. It was too bad that, for the time being, they would have to live behind drawn blinds.

On the door we placed a placard warning that contagious disease had put the house under quarantine. It worked. The Germans took over most of the houses in that quiet street, but they did not enter the infected home of the City Judge.

The following day I had an excellent map made for Oscar, but he did not appear at the meeting-place. I returned to my office. A few minutes later word came that Gunnar, our intermediary wished to see me immediately. I knew where to go. Gunnar was a Norwegian officer who lived as a civilian in town, but he had not laid aside his responsibilities with his uniform. He lived near the church and I found him at our usual meeting place in the church basement.

"It's about the young fellow you are using," he said. "He was to see me yesterday. He was dressed in knickers and a windbreaker, wasn't he?"

"Yes," I answered.

"I fear they have got him. A while ago a van passed down the street. On the floor lay a boy dressed as I have described. His face was shot away. I could not tell for sure who it was, but thought it best to let you know."

Oscar killed—his face shot away! And I had sent him. No, it could not be! He carried no documents on his person.

"Let's wait a while to see. Don't let us talk any more about it now," I said.

I returned to my work, but I froze so that my whole body shivered.

Miss Hansen put her head inside the door.

"I forgot to tell you that a boy was here to see you. He reeked of fish."

"Beloved Hansen, where is he?"

"He took the back stairs to the attic."

Of course it was Oscar with a broad grin across a complete face. He had been delayed. He had to say good-bye to someone.

"Well, if it is a girl again, I give you up for hopeless."

"No, no girl, but I have made a date to go with a fellow who is driving a vanload of coffins to Beidsfjord. I did not think it wise to show myself in town before I went. The van is outside the coffin factory up the street. I was scared. I thought you weren't coming."

Scared? Never in all my sinful life had I myself been so scared. I told him what Gunnar had feared. The body in the van must have been that of a German scout who had been hit by shell-fire from the ships. We knew that the Germans used not only Norwegian uniforms but also civilian clothes.

I was not eager to send Oscar on his way, but he insisted. I gave him his map and bade him farewell. He promised not to return for a while. That promise he kept. The next time I was to hear from him he was serving on board a Norwegian freighter off Canada.

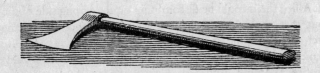

XIII *Thunder in the Mountains*

DURING the next few days we were to hear more from our allies in Håkvik. They had brought up an howitzer on the other side of the mountain and sent heavy shells over the town from time to time. They obviously had established a lookout post on the mountain plateau across the harbour.

The first shots were wild, but those that followed were usually direct and meaningful. Once the range-finding equipment became accurate, more and more German quarters were destroyed. Admittedly, the civilians paid, for the Germans simply moved into new houses; but, as time went on, they felt less and less secure. At night we could hear the patrols singing in the streets, more often as a result of Norwegian brandy than of German courage. In constantly increasing numbers the Germans made use of Norwegian uniforms and civilian clothes. When we protested they pointed to the German emblem, or armband, with the inscription *Deutsche Wehrmacht* and said, "It's easy enough to read, isn't it?"

"Certainly, at bayonet point," we retorted, "but scarcely from the destroyers out in the fjord."

When Finn and Arne sent their men up along the railway line with food and medicines for the evacuated Norwegian families forced to stay in the mountain cottages, the German soldiers mingled with the Norwegian relief workers.

Even Allied shells could be discomfiting on the wrong side of the firing line, but that could not be helped. Our impatience had changed its character. We had come to understand what this war demanded. It would not do merely to rush ashore with guns blazing. Most of us would escape the gun fire. We must wait.

Shells are worse than bombs. They scream more fiercely and come over more regularly. One is given time to dread. The tunnel and the basements again became populated. The old told fairy tales to the young, but the children found what was happening above their heads more exciting and more unbelievable than the legends. Children were most frightened when they saw that their parents were frightened, and most mothers, consciously or unconsciously, realized it. It was the children who kept the women erect and calm, but it was also the children who bound us all to constant caution.

Naturally, we had our casualties among civilians. Accidents happened every day. A city janitor had his head blown off when a shell exploded in the Market Place. During the attack on the German positions at Framnes some of the shells exploded in the city itself.

One morning we heard a shrill scream directly above the City Hall and saw the shells bursting higher up in the city. From the windows we could see smoke from a little house in Street 3. We heard people down in the street shout, "That's Hårek Olsen's house. There were people in the kitchen."

I knew Hårek Olsen. He was a member of the Fire Brigade. In a few seconds a fire engine sped through the street. Soon some of the people returned from the scene.

Half of the house was shot away, but there had not been much of a fire. Yes, there had been people inside. Three young girls in the kitchen, two sisters and a girl friend from the neighbour's. Hårek had been the first to enter. There had been some blood splotches and a few garment fragments on one wall. That was all that was left of them. The father had recognized the garments.

Later in the day, I stopped in at the Fire Station. Olsen was at work again. There was not much that anyone could say in such circumstances, except to ask whether there was anything we could do for him. His white face, hard and tense, shone in the dim workroom. He thanked us, but said there was nothing he wanted except to work. The shell must have gone astray. No one ever heard him say a bitter word against the British.

The next Sunday something similar happened. Five or six women came to the City Hall to ask for food that they might take over to Øyjord. A few days before a motorboat had come from the city with provisions for the population there, but the German soldiers had stolen it.

"But why were not boys sent on this errand?" we asked. "It is fatally dangerous to cross the fjord now."

"We tried," they said, "but the Germans refused to grant permission. They were afraid that boys might board the British ships. Finally we were permitted to take two rowing boats, but only women could go. Most of us have children waiting for us at home."

We loaded the Red Cross wagon with the best provisions we had— flour, beans, and canned goods. We also had a small supply of chocolate for the children, and each of the mothers received a package. Then they left for the shore. Arne asked the station wagon to wait while he ran down to the apothecary shop to get some bottles of cod-liver oil.

He was hardly back when a boy came running over the bridge. He was headed for the City Hall and we heard him shout confused words of excitement.

"There's nothing left of them. They're all dead!"

I saw the men start to unload the wagon and I ran down, only to see it disappear at high speed, Arne and Finn on the running boards. A heap of tarpaulins bounced up and down in the empty truck.

The boy caught his breath enough to tell a fairly coherent story of what had happened. From a few hundred yards away he had seen a group of women by two rowing boats. They had started to load packages into the boats. Suddenly the ships had opened fire. In quick succession two or three shells hit. He had thrown himself behind a huge stone by the road. When he looked up, the women were no longer there, but there were two oblong holes in the sand, a bloody mess, and bits of clothing and flesh spread over a wide area. It was impossible to conceive that these bits had been human beings. He had seen heads without bodies.

The boy could not continue. He began to vomit.

We were still in the street when the Red Cross wagon returned. The driver asked for Mr. Njöten. The men did not know just what should be done. Mr. Njöten emerged from the first-aid station. We agreed he had better take some coffins along.

Later in the day we issued a sort of protocol. There were five caskets. They were numbered, and we indicated who was lying in each of them. But they were sealed before friends and relatives came for them.

We had meant to act in the most practical manner; but there should have been one more casket.

One of the carpenters employed at the reinforcement work in the church basement called later at the City Hall. He had heard that his daughter had been home to inquire about him. She had gone to stay with a family at Øyjord on the day of the invasion and he had felt happy that she was safe. Now he had heard news of the accident at Vasvik and he was anxious about her. She was his one child, only nineteen. Her name was Constance. I knew her. She had been in the group of women that had gone down to the rowing-boats. But her name was not on our list. I showed it to him. He smiled a smile of relief. But the smile suddenly froze when he saw the uncertainty on our faces. We told him to return to work while we started a search for Constance.

We realized that there had been a mistake. It had been impossible to identify the dead or even to know exactly how many women had been in the group. Eye-witnesses thought they had seen five persons before the accident, but now it was too late to do anything. Later, Mr. Njöten told Constance's father that she must have drifted out to sea. The old carpenter wanted to drag for her. He begged for people to follow him at once, but we explained that we dared not risk any more lives. We would find Constance one day so that she might have a proper funeral.

At first we did not discuss the cause of the accident very much. Most of the men could not understand it. The distance had been little more than a mile. The men on the warships must have been able to ascertain that it was not Germans who were working by the two rowing-boats. We heard it said in the air-raid shelters that the shells must have come from one of the German guns up in the mountains. Some people chose to believe this, or, rather, wanted to believe it. The atmosphere was dark and confused.

I felt that the situation must be growing steadily worse, if it could be believed that the shells had been German, when everyone who had seen the marks in the sand must know that the shells had come from the sea.

A group of us met to discuss the incident. We agreed that there was no reason to permit our people to believe that a German shell had caused the tragedy. In most respects the German weapons were superior to our own, but we did have one advantage. We could always dare to tell the truth. And even in this instance it must be possible to make the people realize who was really to blame. The Germans not only walked about in Norwegian uniforms but they made use of civilian clothes and women's clothes when they patrolled the seashore and the railway line. The British had learned of this deception. On the Sunday morning of the accident, however, real Norwegian women had been on the shore.

It was necessary to postpone the funeral for a few days. The Germans had promised to return the church to us. It had long since been agreed that the merchant-navy men quartered there should be shipped home to Germany via Sweden. Finally they were on their way. Since they were civilians, they had received Swedish visas. later, we learned that a German U-boat crew had been smuggled through with them.

The church was packed for the funeral. The parson was living with a colony of evacuees somewhere up along the railway line, so his assistant officiated. He was a small man with a crooked back, but as upright a human character as can be found among men. He tried to make his funeral sermon as subdued as possible, but behind his words there trembled a fire of intense emotion.

Most of the church windows had been blasted away, but the church itself was washed and decorated with the flowers of spring. Graves had been dug in the church garden outside, since the cemetery at the outskirts of Northtown was no longer accessible. The graves had been laid open by the shelling, and our little stone chapel had been blown to bits. Debris covered the graveyard.

It was a sad funeral. Saddest of all was the father of Constance. He did not even have a casket. The pastor performed a beautiful little ceremony in the memory of the young girl. Some flowers were taken from the wreaths to be thrown upon the sea as a last farewell.

On May 13th, Bjerkvik in Herjangen was recaptured by the French Foreign Legion. During the previous night there had been fierce bombardment from the ships. Tromsö Radio had warned the civilian population for days. We saw the village burn and hoped that the peasants had escaped to the woods. The same evening the radio announced Allied victories. Bjerkvik had been cleared of the Germans, and Norwegian forces had recaptured several important positions in the mountains. The next few days we could hear the front creeping steadily in on both sides of the town. We were losing more of our people, both soldiers and civilians, every day.

The tempo became intensified, even in the air. Until now, only a few planes had come over and they had been, for the most part, transport planes, dropping provisions and mail to the German forces.

During the entire siege of Narvik the German troops received mail twice a week. The mail bags floated slowly through the air fastened to small parachutes.

Sometimes the bags were rather heavy. The Germans said they contained Red Cross materials. On one occasion, when a parachute failed to open, a bag fell through the roof of a little house in Frydenlund into an old lady's bedroom. She awoke to find the room filled with cartridges.

Now, it was mostly bombers that came over, huge, grey birds of prey, fighting the ships. The battleship *Warspite* had long since left for more important theatres of war but destroyers constantly roamed the fjord. Often they clung so close to shore that we could wave to them. On one occasion we thought we observed one of them flying a Polish flag.

The German bombers invariably arrived during mid-morning, having probably started at dawn from the German bases. Sometimes we watched aerial combat against the translucent spring sky. The British were obviously making use of a base south of Tromsö. The British planes were fighters, small, and with sharp wings. The Germans attempted to stay away from any dog-fights. They came bursting from the mountains in the direction of the Swedish border into the fjord, but they never succeeded in catching the ships off guard. The vessels were continuously on the move. We could see them rush at top speed, zigzagging towards the open water whenever the planes appeared, and the skies were dotted by smoke rings from the guns. Day after day the performance was repeated. On only one occasion did we see a German plane shot down.

Once, immediately above Framnes, we saw a bomber come down in a spin. It looked as if it had been mortally hit. But, as soon as it was out of the vision of the ships at sea, it levelled off, flew close to the housetops, and disappeared above the ridge.

We could not see the destroyers in the fjord; but, judging from the shelling and bombing, the plane could not have been far out from shore when it took the destroyers by surprise. There were terrific explosions which boded ill for our friends. That evening the German officers boasted of sinking a Polish destroyer. Brandy flowed freely, and we took advantage of the opportunity to strike a not unprofitable bargain involving a green necktie.

A young German lieutenant had visited all the stores in vain seeking a tie that matched his uniform. He was in charge of the petrol supply service. We of the city had to beg for each barrel, since the Germans had taken all our petrol at the first opportunity. Once before he had chided us on the city's poor stocks of neckties. This evening he reiterated his keen disappointment.

He was in high humour, and we said that we would propose a little deal. We would see that he got an exquisite green tie of the best British make if, in exchange, we got a four-door sedan. Several seized cars of this description stood behind the Royal Hotel. The lieutenant was willing, but he refused to allow any record to be made of the transaction.

Both the sedan and the necktie were put to use the same evening. We had our first ride in the sedan with the stout salesgirl from Danielsen's clothing store, who was still able, from hidden stocks, to supply the wants of her old customers.

The following day we used the car to bring guests to an illegal little celebration in the cellar underneath the Fire Station. It was the Seventeenth of May, Norway's Independence Day. We had been forbidden any kind of public gathering, but we might play music in the homes and hoist the Norwegian flag, *Oberleutnant* Poetsch had announced when he called at the City Hall.

"So that the people out in the fjord may see that we feel happy and free?" we had asked.

"You people have still much to learn," the *Ortskommandant* said, shrugging his shoulders as he left.

No, we did not want music or flag ceremonies on this Seventeenth

I

of May. In a way the Germans themselves took care of that for us. Early in the morning we discovered that they had fastened a huge swastika to a temporary flag-pole raised between the cairn stones on the top of Fagernes Mountain. The ships used it as a target for shooting practice all day. White geysers of snow rose at each hit. The distance was more than five miles. In the afternoon a shell blasted the flag-pole and the obnoxious flag disappeared.

It was then that we decided on a little celebration in spite of the German ban. We were the group from the City Hall, Mr. Njöten's Red Cross boys, and some members of the Fire Brigade. It was no real festival but we still had some of the German beer and a few cigarettes.

It looks like a scene from a Russian drama, I thought, as I descended the ladder into the cellar and saw the flickering candles in empty bottles on the unfinished table tops.

We all felt the need of sitting quietly to talk about the things we were experiencing and getting them into some kind of perspective. We sat in the damp cellar and talked about our national history. It was as if we wished to rediscover our own identity and gain strength and confidence from the living past. Ours were treasures that no one could take from us. We had the traditions of an age-old culture, and yet we felt that we were a young nation.

Our thoughts drifted to that one old man who, in his impressive, erect person, represented our nation and our history. We thought of our King. Ever since, thirty-five years before, he had been elected to the throne of Norway, we had thought of him as something to be taken for granted. He was a living part of our Constitution. Perhaps we had not even been conscious of our real affection for this kindly and simple man. His motto —*All for Norway*—was engraved on our money. We had seen it so often that we no longer associated anything specific with it. Now that he was in mortal danger, we began to appreciate his lifelong contribution.

Through Tromsö Radio we had been able to follow him on his journey to the North. His travels lay through the cities and villages laid waste by German bombers. We proudly realized that so long as our King remained free, our flag was not struck. We pledged him our undying allegiance.

We did not, of course, actually say things like these in that darkened room. The more dramatic the realities themselves became, the more inadequate and futile were words to express them. It was our inner mood that whispered this flaming confidence, and it lived in the dim light between us as well as in the songs we quietly hummed together.

On our way home we drifted through the streets in small groups of two or three, so as not to attract undue attention. We met drunken German soldiers celebrating our Norwegian Independence Day by shooting at street cats scared out of their wits. It seemed that we always had to have some shooting going on about us. A whole night of undisturbed sleep none of us had enjoyed since April 9th.

The acrid odour of continuous fires, the loud noise of explosions, sleepless nights, and dazed minds characterized these bright but chilly spring days of 1940. But we were most aware of the bursting shells. We learned to recognize the multiple sounds of modern warfare. We could distinguish the heavy drone of the big bombers from the lighter humming of the fighter planes. We knew the difference between the boom of the naval guns and the sound from the land batteries. The spitfire shrill of the machine guns sounded different when it came from the ships than when it sang between fighting planes over our heads. We heard bombs crash into the sea, leaving half-choked booms in the tense air. And all these sounds were thrown back into the mountains, each in its own fashion. If we were unable to identify any of them immediately we need but wait for the repetition, since the echoes served only to emphasize their peculiarities. This knowledge was useful. We learned to take proper precautions. The piercing whistles from the howitzer at Håkvik put us on special alert, just as does a country telephone ringing one's own call signal.

The danger was not always proportionate to the volume and strength of the sound. The rattling of shell splinters sounded like soft rain, but it was a sound to watch out for. Many were wounded by those terrifying steel splinters with their sharp and jagged surfaces.

One night a new sound was introduced to the fearsome orchestra. Heavy explosions came from the direction of the Iron Ore Company by the piers. They were not preceded by any shrills and seemed to come out of nowhere. They were blasting explosions. At first we were unable to classify them but we soon learned their meaning. The Germans, realizing that they would be unable to hold the town, had begun to blow it up, just as they had blown up their own ships when the sea battle was lost, so that the enemy would have the least possible joy of victory.

Special blasting experts had been shipped in through Sweden in the guise of civilians. They were busy for a week, and we estimated that they destroyed property to the extent of £100,000 a night.

After a few days we succeeded in sending a message to the Swedish Government, advising that the first thing these special "Red Cross Workers" did when they arrived in Norway was to blow up the properties of the Swedish Iron Ore Company in Narvik.

At first the Germans refused to admit that they were committing these acts of sabotage. They blamed it on British shelling, but Director Hoel of the Company sent them lists of their crimes every morning and lodged a protest in the name of the Swedish company. They did not deem the protest worthy of an answer.

Day by day, Mr. Hoel continued to sit in his executive office. He was a powerful personality of about sixty with a heavy but friendly face. He had entered the company service as a young engineer and had supervised the building of these huge piers and workshops which now, step by step, were being blasted into a desolate waste of stone blocks and twisted iron. Each morning, when he looked out of his windows he could see another part of his life's work destroyed. And he would stand in frozen silence at the inconceivable wantonness of the Nazi demons. Every night between twelve and one o'clock the explosions began, and those who had beds to sleep in had to hold on so as not to be thrown out. Now there was some real point to sleeping on the floor.

One by one the expensive electric locomotives were blown up. The night the huge locomotive stalls went up into the air not a single window was left intact in Street 1. The next day the Polish howitzer set the Grand Hotel on fire and British shells hit the Royal. The Royal was not completely demolished but there were holes through the walls and the Germans hurriedly left it.

We investigated the quarters left by the Germans and found a number of things of interest. In one of the offices, papers were scattered about, pay roll lists, and various forms. One of the printed forms was for the recording of details in connection with suicides among German soldiers. We left them, hoping they might some day be filled out. But we took along some articles belonging to the English consular officials. We also picked up some good telescopes, and a kettleful of delightful partridge, evidently intended for the German officers.

That same evening the birds were served with cream gravy at the City Judge's home. Consul Gibbs sat at the head of the table, again in a freshly pressed suit. He promised me a dinner on board one of the British destroyers in the fjord, a promise which he fulfilled a few days later.

We made good use of the German telescopes. Observation posts were set up to follow the military operations. From Oscar's report I had a general idea of how the recapture was going to be effected. There would be a smashing attack and we had best stay out of the line of fire.

Even the Germans evidently expected something to happen. The *Ortskommandant* had lost most of his papers in the fire that swept the Grand Hotel. He had moved into a makeshift office in the Industrial High School opposite the City Hall, and the high degree of efficiency noticeably slackened.

It would be incorrect to say that the Germans had become frightened, but it was obvious that they no longer enjoyed acting the role of masters. They realized that Narvik was about to fall to the British, and the forms of the New Order fell apart, one by one. The *zahlmeister* no longer bothered to fill out the solemn-looking requisitions or to pay in *reichs-kredittenscheine* for what they looted. Even the illusion that it was British shells that exploded in the night they made no effort to maintain.

When the explosion experts carried their oblong boxes into the transformer station by the bridge we arrived on the scene with drawings and charts to prove that the station had nothing to do either with the Iron Ore Company or with the railway, but that it served only the light system of the town itself. And the transformer escaped destruction that night from "the perfidious Albion."

In other ways, too, we could observe the deterioration of the German morale. They treated their own dead in a most appalling manner. One morning our cemetery registrar rushed in to report that the Germans had stuffed their dead into the sewers by the church and that they had taken a grave that was to have been used for a Norwegian funeral. They had crowded the twisted German corpses into a heap and thrown a little sand on them.

We played it up. We protested in the name of the German dead. We submitted a report of a Norwegian funeral for German soldiers in Beidsfjord, including the numbers of the hymns used on that occasion. And now they themselves stuffed their dead into the sewers! Lieutenant Poetsch was somewhat ashamed, though he thought we were making too much fuss about it. But the corpses were removed and the leader of the German funeral gang was sent to the City Hall to offer apologies. He was a small, pale-faced, fat creature under an over-sized helmet. We were very angry, but his appearance and apology at least provided a kind of explanation.

Three times the *Kommandant* had picked a funeral patrol. The first had been wiped out during its work by the chapel. The second had been on its way in a van with six German corpses when a shell from the ships had buried both the cargo and the patrol. Our visitor was responsible for the third patrol. They were just returning with a fresh load from the positions at Framnes when they discovered the convenient newly-dug sewers in the park by the church and decided that it would be most practical not to drive any farther.

"But the Germans themselves set up the battery positions in the cemetery," we pointed out.

The tiny funeral director with the huge helmet insisted that he had not ordered them there. And we believed him.

The sewer incident did not stand alone. The treatment the Germans gave their dead revealed a cynicism that was depressing, but the wounded at Narvik were excellently cared for. The slightly wounded the Germans treated themselves in the hope of getting them back into service as quickly as possible. The severely wounded were sent to our Hospital.

Our energetic Head Surgeon performed marvellous medical feats, often remaining at the operating table the whole day. The Germans held him in such high regard that his name was removed from the list of hostages. They soon discovered that their own doctors were of poor quality. Their medical leader proved himself a thorough ruffian. When we pointed out to him that the Germans were breaking the international Red Cross laws by erecting gun positions in close proximity to the Hospital, he shrugged his shoulders and answered that the Hospital had an unfortunate position.

We received many small bits of information from the Hospital which served to complete the picture we already had of the enemy. The dying soldiers did not make confessions or reveal military secrets, but they did become more human as they neared the threshold of death themselves.

In the Hospital there was a little nurse with a great blonde braid wrapped around her head. Perhaps her name really was Grete. At any rate she spoke German not too badly. She was the object of constant proposals and when she was sure that the suitors were going to die pretty quickly she told them she would think it over.

The Germans really seemed to be in earnest, and to imagine that they were going to bring youthful Nordic Gretchens home with them. One young sub-lieutenant was especially serious. He quoted Heine and talked philosophy, but he could not for a moment believe that Germany could ever commit a wrong. He related that he was a medical student and that in two years he would start practising in a little Bavarian village where his parents owned a great farm. He delivered eloquent philosophical sermonettes. He admitted that things looked pretty ugly and that we simple-minded Norwegians might find it difficult to grasp the New Order and the deeper meaning behind the invasion. What we were now witnessing, he said, was the birth pangs of a New Era. As in all such processes, it was a hideous and bloody spectacle, but when the struggle was over we should see a beautiful and well-formed child. Peace and order would follow. Blond men and women with strong wills would dominate the world. The women of Bavaria would be clothed in French silk and Irish linen and their men would smoke real tobacco and they would go to cinemas and see American films. Perhaps even Heine would once again be recognized when the Jewish financial swindlers had been liquidated. A new, great, light-hearted, happy Germany was rising.

"But what of the rest of the world?" Grete had interrupted. "Besides, I have a sister who is a brunette."

"Even the others will become happy, since they were born to obey. Yes, all will be truly happy in this life, the only life there is. So happy," said the little lieutenant, and died.

The general picture, as pieced together from these incidents related by the nurses, indicated that the Austrian soldiers really felt a certain sense of shame, and that they were grateful for the kind treatment given them. The Germans, on the other hand, remained for the most part closed and hard. They did not talk much, but they protested violently against being placed in the rooms on the top floors.

I visited the Hospital almost every day and it was here that I first met Dr. Kant. He had arrived as a civilian via Sweden and had fussed and fretted about town for several days. We had heard that the German officers bent over backwards to please Dr. Kant, and that he lived alone. At the Hospital he consistently refused to become involved in any discussion of medical matters, although he visited all the rooms regularly and screamed "*Heil Hitler!*"

Dr. Kant was that type of sausage-German who bangs the table when he talks politics and pronounces universal truths, and berates the waiters when there is either too much or too little foam on the beer. An Austrian soldier, who had lost his leg and was not too sure that the Germans would go to the expense of sending him home as return freight, whispered to us that Kant was from the Gestapo. His visit meant that the Devil was loose.

Whether they were related to the "Doctor's" inspiring energy or not, we received other warnings of coming events. Our freedom of mobility was put under new and more severe restrictions. People were driven from all houses that had an open view of the sea. Maps were posted announcing new forbidden zones. The proclamations contained mysterious threats against any trespassing of these areas. We knew perfectly well what they meant. The Germans had planted land mines along the shore in order to render landing attempts suicidal. The maps were dated May 26th.

On the following night, from an attic where we had posted a lookout, came the electrifying news that a whole fleet was steaming into the fjord. The ships were travelling in close formation and at high speed. They were accompanied by planes. It did not look like an ordinary patrol. The news was spread immediately through the secret channels. This time it appeared to be the real thing.

We had braced ourselves for a harassing test before the city again would be free, but the overwhelming fierceness of this attack was beyond either expectation or description. The night was one continuous explosion. The British ships ran in from both sides of the Narvik peninsula. From the roof and the top floors of the Hospital we had veritable ringside seats. That particular night I had happened to call at a late hour and could follow the dramatic action as in a theatre. Even curtains and wings were not missing from the awe-inspiring stage setting. The air was calm. The play of purple on the mountains was softened by light cotton clouds that seemed to cling to the peaks awhile before they let go and melted away into a quiet blue.

At first we thought the landing would be made to the south of the town. The houses on the opposite side of the harbour were kept under fierce British shellfire. Thank God, the civilians had been evacuated. We knew that some small detachments of Germans had been placed there. But to-night house after house was hit and took fire. Soon the burning houses formed a continuous wall of flame along the shore.

Then the shelling shifted to the north. A few shells burst above the public school buildings. I knew that Ellen and Siri were staying at the Head-master's house by the public park. Accompanied by a friend, I comman-deered an ambulance and drove to the house. The exodus was accom-plished in a few minutes, despite the delay caused by the teacher's wife who insisted on bringing along her fat little dog, which was rushing about, insane with fright. Just as we returned to our observation post in the Hospital, the Headmaster's house was hit.

The shellfire was now concentrated on the north side of town, espe-cially the vicinity of Vasvik harbour. Shells flew like shafts of fire through the houses and we feared the worst, since only the lower part of town had been completely evacuated. The Germans had some small-calibre guns on the mountain slopes. On the Iron Ore Company grounds an anti-aircraft gun was firing in the direction of Ankenesstrand. This meant that the Poles were working their way down towards the sea. Otherwise, the Ger-mans were concentrating their fire on Øyjord peninsula. They did not seem to be so much concerned about the ships as about the troops on the other side. We saw a few direct hits on the homes around the small ferry dock. The German gunfire, however, grew steadily weaker. One by one their guns were being silenced.

One of the British destroyers went close to shore a little inside Rom-bakken and opened fire against a wooded ridge that levelled off into the sea. Geysers of trees and earth shot into the air after each hit.

Then, just before the summer midnight, attacking troops came in small landing barges from the direction of Øyjord. We realized that there would be hand-to-hand fighting north of the town. That area was free of land mines. We remained standing at the Hospital windows, shivering with excitement. Shell fragments spattered against the walls and made us duck, but we did not move away. The spectacle was too fascinating to miss.

Wounded soldiers crept out of their beds. Some British patients whom we had kept in a separate room also came limping out. We had reported them as hopeless, but there they were, and they brought along field glasses they had managed to keep hidden. The glasses circulated from nurses and doctors to us visitors and on to the German and British wounded. The Germans realized that they would be prisoners by morning and became more ill and more polite as the night wore on.

Now we saw the attacking troops disembark. We could hear the machine guns and the quick explosion of hand grenades. For a while it looked as if the Germans would hold the forest, but suddenly their fire lessened. Within an hour after the landing the din abated. The recapture of Narvik had taken a good four hours.

We saw German soldiers withdraw to the south of the town. A party crept out of the Telegraph Office and broke up into small groups. One by one we could see them moving down Street 1 and farther on towards Beidsfjord. The last group of Germans to leave town blew up the gun position on the Company grounds. It had stood in the vicinity of a huge coal supply which also caught fire. That was our last coal supply.

The next morning, except for the wounded in the Hospital, not a single German was left in town. But, as yet, our troops had not begun to move in. A strange mood of uncertainty lay over the city, and we were all extremely sleepy.

"You all look pale and happy, like a bride at the breakfast table," Mr. Njöten commented as he drove by with a load of German corpses he had picked up around the Railway Station.

Later that morning I went for a walk in the direction of the cemetery. In a forest grove the French Foreign Legionnaires lay in position. I waved my arms and aired my French, such as it was. A colossus of a professional warrior approached me. He said that they had been ordered to halt for a while. I had, therefore, better return to town and ask the people to remain quiet. The Legionnaires would be coming in very shortly. To make it quite certain he gave me a kiss of joy on both cheeks. Damn it, I thought, that those Germans have bought up all the shaving cream!

The Frenchmen came, graciously arriving second to the Norwegian troops, who had taken part in the storming of the town. The first blond Norwegian boy that marched into town was the young son of the town baker. We took him in a bannered car to his parents, who embraced him with dough sticking to their forearms. They had had no news of him since the start of the war.

Then we drove to the Judge's house to fetch Consul Gibbs and his colleagues. British, French, and Polish flags waved on the car. We drove up and down Street 1. The Norwegian flag again floated above the City Hall and it was more beautiful than ever before.

XIV   *Abandoned Victory*

W E were free again. People emerged from the cellars, and there were
      smiles and hilarious reunions. The Day had arrived at last. It was
a Sunday. The only pity was that we were so sleepy that we could not
enjoy it to the full. Even so, there was not going to be much sleeping.

We inquired about all that had happened at the front. The Norwegian
soldiers, who had been in the thick of the mountain fighting for weeks,
gave vivid descriptions of the battles around the town. They had slept in
snow huts and had gone without warm meals for days. Many casualties
had been suffered from the German planes until they learned how to take
cover, and the Germans had employed all kinds of trickery, including the
wearing of Norwegian uniforms and the forced use of the civilian population. German misuse of civilians and of the Red Cross sign had been
especially bad at Gratangen, where the Norwegians had sustained heavy
losses.

In other battle zones, too, the civilians had suffered greatly. At Bjerkvik,
the peasants had moved to the woods as a result of the radio warning; but,
when nothing happened, they had gone back to their homes on the shore.
Many were killed during the recapture.

The actual recapture of Narvik cost one hundred and fifty soldiers. The
French Foreign Legion and the Norwegian forces shared equally in the
losses. Miraculously, of the civilian population in town only a few were
wounded, and but one man was killed, a young sailor who had been
spared when the *Norge* went down on April 9th.

We visited the Foreign Legionnaires, who had taken over the earth
caves which the Germans had dug at Framnes. They intended to establish
new positions outside the town the same night. They were made up of

soldiers of many nations and had come from the fighting in Africa to the war above the Arctic Circle. The Colonel himself was from Vienna. He was enjoying a cup of tea outdoors with his officers when we arrived. An upturned crate was being used for a table. We asked him whether there was anything we might do, at least to the extent of furnishing better quarters. He thanked us, but said that he preferred to sleep in the open with his soldiers. They had not brought any anti-aircraft guns with them and thought it best to camp in the woods back of the town. He wished only some brandy for his wounded and graves for his dead.

Late the next evening a Mass was held in the church. Our young parson and the French army priest officiated. Three coffins decked with flags were placed before the altar. They represented the fallen French, British, and Norwegian. In the cemetery there were rows of caskets. They were all placed in a common grave. Soldiers, officers, and civilians thronged the place. We did not know one another and had difficulties with our differences in language. Yet around this great open grave we felt as one great family. Its name was Liberty. It could be found all over the earth and it was powerful and numerous, if only it could find place and opportunity to muster its powers. Here, under the Midnight Sun, we had answered a common call and we had won our first land victory. The dead had not died in vain.

The following day we were given to understand that it would be wise to move women and children out of the town. The Germans had bombed Norwegian towns before, where there had been neither soldiers nor forts. Narvik would undoubtedly be attacked with the utmost fury.

It was hard to get boats, and people were not too willing to leave their homes, now that we had recaptured our town and again were free.

Commander Askim organized an air alarm system with the survivors from the *Norge* and the *Eidsvold*. The church bells were used as warning signals, the heavy bell for danger and the small one for the all-clear.

One night a French gun exploded, and questions were raised about fifth columnists. We knew of no quislings except Sundlo, but perhaps the Germans had left behind some spies in civilian clothes. We got news of one of them. Before the recapture of the town, an Austrian soldier had been befriended by a Norwegian family when he had insisted that he was an anti-Nazi. He declared that he would desert, and his Norwegian friends had given him a suit and hidden him in their cellar during the last days of the fighting. He had remained in town a few days after the liberation. Now he had disappeared.

The old trickery once more, playing on our good, dumb, democratic hearts!

Again we had contact with the world outside. One morning there was a long-distance call from the Norwegian War Department, now stationed at Tromsö. We received congratulations and instructions. I recognized the voice. It was my father's. He had arrived in the North with the Royal party.

Congratulations poured in. It was not in vain that we had been the first city to be recaptured by the Allies. From Tromsö came representatives of the Government Press Service. Again there were interviews and radio greetings. Swedish journalists arrived. They were especially interested in learning whether we had any quislings.

The incident concerning Consul Gibbs and the partridge was described in detail by the optimistic radio station at Tromsö. Everyone was supremely sure that final victory had been won in the Narvik sector.

We also had military visitors. A British General and an Admiral dropped in on the town. The Admiral was a Lord and looked as friendly and as dignified as the distinguished gentleman on the label of old three-star brandy. The Foreign Legionnaires held a brief parade for the visitors in Vasvik. His Lordship was slightly impatient, as though the waiting tea was getting cold. German bombing planes circled above our heads. Had they known what distinguished persons we were on that battered ferry dock that morning, they most certainly would not have limited themselves to the bombing of ships. The guests departed safely and the Legionnaires returned to their positions.

Soon we could follow again the well-known drama in the fjord, the zigzagging destroyers in combat with the bombing hawks.

A few days later Polish officers and soldiers descended in triumph on the town. They had taken the mountain to the south. Beidsfjord had been cleared of Germans. Norwegians who had assisted the Poles said that they had fought like madmen. For them it had evidently been more important to kill Germans than to secure a tactical position.

"Here in Norway the Germans have behaved like angels," they said, "but just wait. If you have anything more to do with them, the picture will be different."

We were in a strange position. We heard that Bodö had been bombed and taken. The general military position throughout the country appeared to be hopeless. In certain southern districts, where small detachments refused to give up in the woods and on the mountains, guerilla warfare continued. But it could only be a question of time before the Germans had "mopped up," as they loved to express themselves.

Admittedly, their attempt to use quislings had failed; there were not enough quislings. The Norwegian Administration at Oslo had been taken over by a Council of leading officials. Even that makeshift arrangement seemed to be but a mutual bargaining for time.

In the Narvik sector the picture was reversed. The remainder of General Dietl's army was deadlocked in the mountains along the Iron Ore Railway behind the town. The Germans were flanked on three sides and would soon have to choose between annihilation and retreat into neutral Sweden, where they would be demobilized and interned. We knew that there were armed forces of considerable size across the border.

At first, we were a little bitter against our Swedish brethren, but later we understood better. Like ourselves, Sweden was ill-prepared. She was admittedly a larger nation, with a stronger military machine, but she had sent the main part of her munition supply to Finland the previous winter. Sweden could not have offered us any assistance.

Then the birds came over with eggs earmarked for Narvik. In the first serious air bombardment they attempted to destroy the offices of the civil administration. Because of broken windows and holes left by shell splinters from the Polish howitzer, we had moved our offices from the City Hall to the near-by Fire Station. The latter was a partly-finished brick building. The cellar and the first floor were completed, but during the depression we had run out of funds, and, since the remainder of the building had been planned as a community hall, we had put our dreams into the drawer with the blueprints and put a temporary roof over the unfinished part.

Several hundred persons were in the air-raid cellar when the bombs fell. They exploded in the section across the railway tracks. That block of houses went up in flames, but we succeeded in rescuing some of the wounded. With Finn, I drove a van to the Hospital, carrying an old woman who had half a leg torn off, and an old acquaintance, an engineer who only a few moments earlier had been in our office. He complained of loss of sensibility in the lower part of his body, but spoke calmly and cheerfully during the trip to the Hospital. He died on arrival. His spine was broken.

We realized that we must evacuate as many people as possible. The boats we had commandeered held no more than twenty to thirty persons each. We telephoned all the sheriffs in the surrounding districts, but they could tell us only that all their boats had sailed away. The Chief of Police at Harstad promised to send some fishing vessels as soon as he could find them.

One night we held a meeting at the Iron Company office. It was near the tunnel, which now was looked upon as the only safe place in town. During the meeting it was reported that an Englishman was outside and wished to come in. I went out to see him. He was a young man in a raincoat and a British helmet. He spoke Norwegian with an English accent. The visitor introduced himself as Lieutenant Job—Patrick Job. He wanted to talk to us about the evacuation. He had boats.

I asked him to come in. If he had been sent from heaven he could not have appeared at a more opportune moment. He informed us in a strange, primitive Norwegian that he belonged to the Royal Navy but that he had been commissioned to work with the evacuation of civilians. He had rented half a hundred fishing vessels in Lofoten. The boats would come in the fjord in small groups of five or six. As identification signals they had red and white paint on the prows and flew the flags on the bows instead of on the stern. They had completed the civilian evacuation of Bodö. Now it was Narvik's turn. Seven vessels lay ready to sail at Øyjord; they would have to depart within two hours. It was now about midnight, but it was not easy to get people ready. He realized that the time was not too good, but speed was imperative. He must have three or four hundred women and children on board these boats.

He had seated himself on the side of the Director's desk and dangled his sea boots in seeming embarrassment as he talked. When he removed his helmet, he looked even younger, with his unruly blond hair and an open smile on a sunbaked face.

I suppose that most of us unconsciously compared him with the young officers who had just been driven out of Narvik. They had been hard-bitten warriors with plans of world conquest. Here was a college youth, still a trifle timid at being an officer. He had been put ashore to try to find ways and means to be of assistance. This was the youth of that "decadent" England which took loss and defeat until it found a way to gain victory.

We asked him how the war was going.

"Absolutely rotten, but the problem now is how to get these boats going."

"Where are they bound?"

He did not know, but he had made arrangements with a man who sat with a telephone on a pier somewhere out in the fjord at a place called Kjeldbotn. The boats would pass and call to him, and he, having contact with the local sheriffs in the islands, would announce the destination to each individual boat.

We liked Patrick Job. We sent vans to all the air raid cellars and took out the women and children. Lieutenant Job went to Vasvik and waved a huge yellow flag. Boat after boat moved across the fjord and loaded its cargo of sleepy children and excited mothers. Each boat had a leader, who, during the voyage, was to make a complete list of his passengers and be responsible for them on arrival.

Job stood on the pier, smiled to the children, cursed the skippers, and waved his flag. We furnished the cargo, but it was considerably more than two hours before the last families had sent back the superfluous suitcases with table linen and silver spoons. Each woman could take along only what she herself could carry. The evacuation was to continue the next night.

On the way home we asked Job whether he had any quarters and luggage, and also where he had picked up his Norwegian, which was serviceable even though it was not academically impeccable. He told us that on his holidays he had often gone fishing along the Norwegian coast and had learned it from the fishermen. He had had a sea-going sailboat before the war. He had not arranged for any quarters and would like to get a place to sleep. He had brought along a toothbrush and had a pair of clean socks in his pocket.

The next day at noon we paid a visit to Consul Gibbs in the City Judge's home, where we were met by an atmosphere of deep gloom. It was obvious that there had been bad news. The news was confidential, but we understood that it had to do with the situation in Norway.

As we left, Job suggested that we go for a ride through the town. There was no reason to take the sorrows in advance. We would hear soon enough, and there was much to do in the meantime. And what did a little bad news, more or less, matter?

We drove to the ore docks. The scene was one of utter chaos. There must have been more than thirty shipwrecks in the harbour, and the tops of masts and parts of ships protruded from the water. Along the docks lay more blasted and desolated ships. *Jan Wellem* lay with less than half its hull above water. We went on board. The spacious cabins were empty. There was not as much as a pair of dirty socks left.

We returned to the office. The Administration must be kept up to date. A meeting of the City Council was to be held that day. The various arrangements and disposals that had been made would have to be reported for approval. In the midst of our meeting the heavy church bell began to sound a warning of enemy bombers. But the planes were on their way to a destination farther north. It was going to be a quiet day, after all. Other places were about to taste the fury of Nazi destruction and desolation.

At the close of the meeting a Swedish journalist appeared with the message that the Swedish Red Cross was ready to receive Norwegian children. He had personally come through the German lines and told us that the Germans would permit groups of ten a day to pass through, including the grownups who were taking care of the children. The Germans were probably glad to have a little respite from the fighting. We knew they were hard pressed and were being forced to retreat farther and farther into the mountains. The spring thaw had come in the higher regions and the terrain was not too favourable for troops under fire. We organized special groups of evacuees to go inland, mostly persons with families or relatives in Sweden.

The Sunday following the recapture of Narvik we had our first spring day of 1940. It was almost hot, and the streets were snowbare and dry. The trees had the faint green veil. It was June 2nd. During the night we had evacuated the last children. I had waved good-bye to Ellen and Siri. They had carried one suitcase and a small bag of bedding, plus old Trine. Trine had a dirty bandage around her head and a big safety pin in her stomach to keep what was left of the sawdust inside. The children had been playing bombing attack in the park.

Well into the morning German planes came over. There were twenty in all. These were the planes meant for us. They circled in at a low altitude in the absolute assurance that we were without anti-aircraft guns. The ships had left. We could only sit and wait and take it. We harboured no illusions. This time they had come to destroy the town and "lower the morale." They started with Street 1 and worked their way uptown. In Frydenlund they blasted the new Police Chamber, which was housed in a private home near the church. They also attempted to hit the entrance to the air-raid tunnel near the Iron Company. Job coolly contributed the observation that, if it were hit, not one of the five hundred persons inside would survive. The tunnel had no gates, and the air pressure would hit inwardly. Even so, there were no other shelters that were secure except against splinters.

We stood the test. I inspected all the big cellars and I saw no one who had lost his self-control. Calmness was something we had continually stressed. When people had come to the City Hall sobbing or whining they had been kept in the corridors until they could control their emotions. Now only men and unmarried or childless women were left. The young girls who remained were mostly nurses or volunteers in the public soup kitchens.

The more people there were in the air-raid shelters the higher the spirits seemed to be. Some spoke as loudly as possible to prevent others from listening to the screams of falling bombs and counting the explosions.

The bombing lasted for two hours. It seemed to be mainly five-hundred-pound bombs that were dropping on us, interspersed with incendiaries. Fires started wherever they hit and the conflagration spread. Heavy aerial machine-gun fire accompanied the bombing. In a defenceless city machine-gun fire along with the bombing does produce its intended effect of utter helplessness. It seemed that there was no limit to the savagery the Germans were prepared to use on civilians.

At length the British fighting planes arrived and we had an opportunity to attempt to save what was still left of the town. To extinguish the conflagration was impossible. We could only try to limit the fire and remove as much furniture and food stores as was possible from the threatened houses. The fire leapt from building to building and the heat was so intense that all wooden material seemed to melt away. We hoped that the fire would be arrested at Danielsen's brick building, at least momentarily, so that we might use the fire hose more effectively, but the fire was too fierce. The windows were shattered and within a few seconds the fire raced through the building and started on the next.

We dynamited the last house by the Market Place and managed to save the northern part of town. Everyone who remained in the city took part in salvaging all kinds of movables, which were piled in the streets and parks—furniture and clothing, dentist chairs, canary birds, and canned goods. There was no looting.

The entire business district was destroyed. The State liquor store burned down with all doors locked. We did not permit one bottle to be spared. When matters quieted somewhat, we counted our casualties. We had escaped miraculously. Only three persons had been killed. Because of the gradual intensification of bombing and incendiarism over several weeks, we had become quite efficient in taking precautionary measures. Not for one moment was there panic among our citizens.

In the midst of the conflagration we reported to Tromsö. My father was on the wire once more. I told him that Ellen had left and that she would attempt to communicate with him.

Bombing could never break us, but it did create a certain disturbance. In the air-raid shelters and in the tunnel the spirits were high, but people began to tire. Excitement keeps one's courage up, but as soon as the tension is relaxed the reaction sets in. Then one is overcome by a great weariness and can go to sleep anywhere.

That night Job sent a few boatloads of elderly people out of town.

Young men were going into military service; others, able to work, remained to repair the railway and the public dock. We organized a Norwegian Military Police and had a Norwegian Commanding Officer.

The men of the Foreign Legion came into town only at intervals. One evening I met their Colonel in the street. He expressed his gratitude for some brandy we had sent him from the Hospital, and asked whether we could get him a new banner. The old one had been destroyed in battle. He provided a drawing to be used as a pattern, but it was anything but easy to find the proper material or someone to sew it. Finally, the wife of one of the engineers contributed a formal dress that she thought might be changed into a Foreign Legion standard.

Strange indeed were the days that followed. The fighting in our own front sector progressed very satisfactorily, but the news from Belgium, Holland, and France was heartbreaking. Rumours began to spread that the Allied troops in the mountains were about to be evacuated. We refused to believe it. Half the victory was already won. The Germans were being pressed ever closer to the border. In this sector, at least, there would be a complete victory. A British General Staff officer came to inform himself of the spirit. We assured him that our spirit was good, but said that it would be even better if we had a battery of anti-aircraft guns. Other foreign officers arrived and asked strange questions. We began to put things together. The skipper of one of the evacuation boats returned and told us that the British had begun to embark at Harstad. Our officers had no information.

On June 6th, the Foreign Legion standard was completed. The formal dress was certainly going to a dance this time! The banner was rust red and green and carried the Legion's emblem on one side and a greeting from Narvik on the other. I looked up some fine French words in a dictionary. It would, perhaps, be quite proper to make a short speech. The Norwegian liaison officer assigned to the Legion dropped in and I asked his advice. He said he had information for us. The city was to be given up within the next twenty-four hours. The Allies were withdrawing their troops. I gave him the banner and asked him to deliver it.

We sat around the office desks at the Fire Station. We did not say much. Someone asked whether the war was over, whether we had lost. We did not know. No, the war could not have been lost. We decided to empty the town and go north. The northernmost part of the country was still free.

Job returned. He told us that he had called all his ships back and that the next day would be the last.

I called Tromsö. I realized that it was impossible to make any further inquiries by telephone, but we did receive powers to continue the evacuation. My father had not had any word from Ellen and Siri. He implored me not to permit myself to be caught.

That night the Foreign Legion fought overtime along the length of the railway line. We heard that Norwegian troops had counterattacked farther inland. The following morning the Legionnaires were in town. I met the Colonel at the dock. It was evident that he deplored the situation as though it had been a personal humiliation, but he remained a gentleman to the last. Our banner would fly in new battles, he said, and he wanted to make a return gift. He pointed to some fifty mules that had been used in munition transport. It was impossible to take the animals back to France. Perhaps we could take them over and, preferably, eat them as quickly as possible. Mule stew in hot sauce was not too bad, he said. We promised to do our best, although there were other tasks which required more immediate attention.

Perhaps it made no difference, but we made it a point of honour to maintain order to the last minute. The Hospital personnel, the parson, and a few other persons were to remain with the wounded. We had to bring the city records out. As much food as possible must also be taken along. We were interrupted by a last bombardment, but not many bombs were dropped on this trip. Job had set the deadline for departure at 8 p.m. He said he would accompany me in a small boat. The deadline was postponed to 10 p.m. There was a little time left for last-minute instructions, but the telephone went dead; the personnel at the station had gone. I threw the receiver on the desk. Our city was no longer functioning.

Job arrived in a van and we drove the public archives down to the dock. There was a strong smell of soot and dirt in the air. Street 1 was a meaningless ruin. It was strange that so little could remain of the houses. There was nothing left but a layer of brown powder and rubble, with chimneys standing here and there like barren trees in a nightmare. Bedding and crushed furniture littered the street.

When we arrived at the pier, most of the ships had gone. The last of the military were being shipped. We boarded a small boat and sailed out into the fjord.

Narvik—the young, vigorous town! Only two months ago we had been happy there. Perhaps we had failed to realize how fortunate we had been. Ten thousand citizens had lived there. Now but fifty remained. The smoke from the last scenes of the devastation drifted out toward us in a tired and hopeless farewell.

We travelled all night. Occasionally German planes circled overhead, but we knew we were not a significant target, so we moved steadily along. In the early morning we approached Harstad, the white little town on Norway's greatest island, Hindö, immediately north of Lofoten. Job informed me that the British Headquarters were there. He thought that they had already been given up, but some of their ships should still be there.

We entered the harbour as a huge troop transport was leaving, a black steamer as large as the Norwegian transatlantic liners. A British destroyer was drawing in its anchor. This was Lieutenant Job's ship. We drew alongside and he climbed on board. He asked us to wait. In a few moments he returned to the rail accompanied by the commanding officer. The officer expressed his gratitude for the treatment of the British Consul and his staff. Now they were outward bound for England. He had orders to take me along if I wished to come. It might be a wise thing to do, he added.

No, I must go North, I told him. Our Government was in Tromsö. I waved good-bye. Job threw his camel's-hair coat down to me. It was a kind of parka, the type worn by British naval officers.

The fishing boat cast off, and the destroyer lashed the water with its propellers.

We proceeded to town. Here and there we could see the effect of bombs, but the town was not badly damaged. We asked people on the dock whether many Narvik evacuees had arrived.

Yes, but not during the last few days.

A fisherman who made his boat fast next to ours told us that he was from Kjeldbotn. The evacuation boats from Narvik had sailed by there. They had seemed to steer north of Harstad. Many rumours were abroad. Had many been killed, he asked. Was there anything left of the town?

Well, there were a few blocks of houses left, and we did not have too many dead. How had it been in Kjeldbotn? Had they seen the naval battles?

He became excited.

Yes, indeed! They fought right off the dock. A hailstorm of shell splinters had fallen inland.

Had there been any accidents?

No, nothing worth mentioning. Some cattle had been killed in the fields, and an old maid up on the ridge. She had been taking care of an old bachelor who had been dying for years. She was to inherit him, people said. There had been a last will. All in vain, now.

"Her name was Amanda?" I said.

Yes, something like that. Was I that well acquainted in Kjeldbotn?

He wished us Godspeed, and we continued north. On our way we saw the destroyers far out at sea. They were westward bound.

About noon we arrived in Tromsö. The stevedores said that the King and the Cabinet had left during the night on board the last British man-of-war out of Tromsö but that some officers and officials had been left behind.

In the improvised Governmental offices everything was quiet. Only a few elderly officials remained, well-known names from Oslo. I delivered my report and was advised to go abroad. Two planes were scheduled to leave for Finland in the afternoon. Perhaps I might secure a place in one of them.

In the evacuated War Department I found a letter from my father with Ellen's new address. He had left for London with the Royal party. The war would be continued from abroad.

Later, I met friends, among them Tor Gjesdal, who had visited Narvik as the representative of the Government Press Office.

No, the war was anything but over. He had been too late to go with the British destroyers. Now he was on his way to Finland. Did I wish to join him?

And I met Viggo Hansteen, the attorney for the National Trade Unions. We were old friends. He intended to stay. He had had no military training and felt that he would be of greater use inside Norway. There were untold difficulties to be faced. Some had to be there to meet them. There was no question in his mind about his choice.

At first, my own course was not too clear. Perhaps one day I would be forced to leave, but just now it was impossible. There was endless confusion. I must find my family and some of our friends from Narvik. We must make some plans for the future. Our people were scattered all through the islands and in the fjords.

I met a young engineer from Narvik who had a car and petrol, and he expressed his willingness to take me with him. We ferried to the mainland and drove south. We slept for a few hours on a farm and continued our journey the next morning.

In the morning we reached Sætermoen, which had been one of the most important inland military centres during the war. The British forces had had their air field in its vicinity. The field was now blown up and the depots were emptied, but groups of Norwegian soldiers drifted along the roads or sat on the side of the highways, waiting for the final demobilization order. They knew that the Norwegian Commander-in-Chief, General Ruge, had gone to arbitrate with the Germans. He had decided to remain with his soldiers. There was no ammunition left. A friend from the Military Police told me that the boys had received the news the day before. They had already guessed as much.

There had never been much military enthusiasm among these sons of Northland farmers and fishermen; no one had imagined that the military conscription we had maintained would ever be put to use. But now they had wept in sheer anger. Some of them had shaken their fists in the faces of the officers, enraged because they could not fight on.

"But the British must have ammunition!" they cried.

There was small comfort for them in the reply that the British would now have to leave to defend their own country.

We had to move on. On the way to the Coast we drove through an evacuated French camp. In contrast to the British, the French troops had not been able to bring themselves to destroy everything behind them. In Sallangen we saw an old factory building filled with food stores and uniforms being looted by Laplanders. We saw Laplander boys drinking brandy from French helmets. They literally waded in biscuits and strange cheeses. It was the only example of looting we observed throughout the whole war. Nauseated and sick, we drove on.

In the middle of the night we arrived at a ferry landing, where we left the car. A fisherman rowed us out to an island where Ellen and Siri were to have sought refuge. Perfect order was being maintained on the island. Ellen and Siri had reached it safely. The sheriff knew where each family was staying. We found the house, and got food and sleep.

After a rest of two days a small party of us sailed for Harstad. We had heard that as yet there were no soldiers there. We knew a few people in the town and obtained a cabin near-by where Ellen stayed with Siri while I visited with various groups from Narvik. Our plan was to open a Narvik office in Harstad. The public schools were being used as havens for refugees. Everyone was inquiring about families or relatives. Through the radio we had instituted a makeshift information service.

Harstad had been a military centre throughout the war, but had never been the scene of any direct action. Even the German planes kept cautiously away from Harstad, since the British had destroyers and anti-aircraft artillery stationed around the town.

We heard that Svolvær, too, was undamaged. The German fish buyer, Herr Köehln, had been extremely zealous, even though no occupation troops had appeared. He had tried to get into Narvik but had been arrested by the Norwegian Police and returned to Svolvær. When he was informed that his Norwegian sweetheart had been taken into custody, he committed suicide, acting with typical German thoroughness and Aryan taste by placing his head under the circular saw in the prison carpenter shop.

Most of our beautiful coastal steamers had been sunk during the war. Whether or not they had been used as troop transports had made no difference. One of them had been bombed by German planes even though it carried wounded and flew Red Cross flags from all masts. The *Nord Norge*, the pride of Narvik, was also sunk. The steamship companies now began to lease fishing vessels to start the traffic anew.

Life along the coast was going to begin again, but no one knew under what conditions.

XV   *Escape*

ON June 15th we held a meeting in the ticket office on the dock at Harstad to discuss the problem of sending the evacuees home. The Narvik radio had ordered the workers to return. We felt that we had better await developments.

When I came out of the office, the dock was crowded with soldiers. One of the local steamers had arrived with troops. They wore Norwegian uniforms, but I recognized some of them as Germans I had seen at Narvik. I walked rapidly toward town.

Now I would have to make a definite decision in my own case.

Suddenly a squad of soldiers came alongside and stopped me. They took me to the Nobel Hotel, a three-story, wooden building close to the pier, and set me in a chair in the lobby. Captain Reichmann had spotted me from a hotel window and ordered that I be brought to him immediately.

The Captain himself came into the room, his face like a thundercloud.

"We have some very interesting information about you, Mr. Mayor," he said. "You are under arrest."

Between two soldiers I was taken into the dining-room. A young officer placed himself at the door. I heard the Captain conferring with someone in the lobby about getting a prison cell for a British spy.

I tried to appear indifferent and calm. The little dining-room was in a corner of the hotel and had windows to the street and to a back yard where there were small storage shacks. It was on the first floor. There was a high cellar beneath. I walked about the room and looked at the pictures on the walls. A lady with a parasol and a coquettish smile hung in a gold frame next to the window facing the back yard. The window was open. Across the room there was a bar, with bottles and postcards, and behind it I saw that there was a stairway leading down to the cellar. The two soldiers remained standing in the middle of the floor. I walked across the room and made another study of the lady beneath the sun umbrella. She had an idiotic smile. Next to the picture hung a mirror. I was pale, and my smile was not very convincing either. Down in the yard a young boy was opening a barrel. He looked up. I nodded as meaningfully as I could, and he understood that I wanted something. I managed to whisper down to him for God's sake to get me a taxi. It must wait for me in the second cross street to the north.

One of the sentries came over and closed the window. I sat down at the bar and lit a cigarette. We could hear more soldiers drive up from the dock. They had apparently already got some vans. The sentries became curious. They both turned their backs on me and looked out of the windows to the street.

"Now or never," I thought, as I ran quickly around the bar. Like lightning I was down the cellar stairs. From the cellar into the yard took no time. Now, if only I didn't make a fatal mistake between the storehouses! I was lucky, and got round the block and into the street on the other side. The car was waiting in the right spot. I threw myself on the floor and we sped away.

We picked up Ellen and Siri at the cabin. I made a brief explanation in a frantic hurry. The Narvik archives and an already-packed knapsack were flung into the car, and we were on our way with greater haste than dignity.

North of town there was a crossroad. Should we choose the shore route towards the sound to the mainland or the road leading across the islands toward the ocean? We chose the latter.

Half a year later I met a young airman in the Royal Norwegian Legation in Washington who told me that he had been in Harstad on that same day. He said that the Germans had stopped all traffic across the sound and searched for us in vain in all boats headed for the mainland. We had been fortunate.

On the other side of Hindö we arranged with a fisherman to take us to an island still farther off shore. I knew there was no telephone there, but there was a small fishing harbour. An even, fine fog drifted in from the sea and even a few hundred yards out we were lost from observers ashore. We rested a few hours above the little harbour, but as soon as a fishing vessel made a call I rushed down to make an arrangement with the crew, in this case an old man and a youngster.

Would they take the three of us for a little sightseeing trip around Lofoten? I was a Life Insurance Inspector.

Yes, they could do that.

We travelled outward among still more distant islands. At a certain place we stopped to leave behind the box of records for safe keeping and to give some orders. Then we set the course south for Lofoten. It was a good boat, with a well-kept cabin in the bow. There was a small stove and a shining copper coffeepot. In the cupboard were coffee and bread. Siri played on deck with some of the great green glass balls that fishermen use to keep their nets afloat. The sun shone over a calm sea. I talked with the skipper.

This was a very special inspection trip that I was taking, I said.

He understood. But he did not have enough oil for any extended trip, unless we stopped at Svolvær.

No, I did not like Svolvær. Could we not go via Vestfjorden into one of those deep fjords that go in almost to the Swedish border?

That would take a good ten hours, but it was possible, to be sure.

Ellen wanted to know what we planned to do. Could not she and Siri go ashore somewhere? It might be easier for me to get through alone. The Germans would be everywhere by this time. A woman and a little girl would make identification too easy. Siri was tired and fretful. She wanted to go ashore. We had forgotten Trine, which did not help matters. I said we had plenty of time to devise a plan. This would probably be the last trip we would have among the islands for a long time. We might as well sit and enjoy it.

We passed through Troldfjorden. Tourists had come from all over the world to see this crooked channel that the ocean had washed into existence between the mountains. It was the most exquisite beauty spot in all Lofoten. Each moment the mountains seemed to be closing in before us. But, suddenly, around a headland, the fjord went on again, until, at last, there were no more mountains. It was as if a curtain had gone up before an orchestra of sea gulls. The open ocean lay before us, somnolent and calm, breathing lightly in the red sunshine.

It was not long before we saw the mountains in Lofoten proper.

I pointed out the Vågakallen to Siri.

But it was nothing but a black mountain, she said.

Yes, now it looked like that. But once upon a time, very long ago, it had been a real giant, who played in the sea and owned all the mountains up here. When he became old he decided to marry and settle down. He knew of a beautiful maiden in the Helgeland mountains. She was called Lekamöya, the playful maiden, and she was the most beautiful woman on the whole coast. The Våga giant wanted her for his wife. But Hestmannen, the Horseman, a younger giant who rode a proud horse in the ocean, loved her too, and wanted to keep her for himself. When he heard that the old giant was going to propose to her, he realized that he must act with great haste. So the Horseman saddled his horse and rode south so furiously that the sea churned about him. Then the Våga giant saw that time was getting short and he became very angry. But he could not get under way so quickly, so he took his great bow and sent an arrow singing after Hestmannen. The arrow went through the Horseman's hat and carried it off, and it landed way out in the ocean.

Of course, this was long, long ago, even before there were men or boats up here. But we could still see the angry Våga giant in the mountain, and, if we went farther south, we could see Hestmannen riding hatless in the sea, while his hat lies floating out on the ocean. That is a beautiful little island called Torghatten, and there is still a big hole through the mountain made by the arrow of the Våga giant.

"Can't we go down and pick it up for him?" Siri asked, half asleep.

No, we had no time now, and our boat was too small anyway. We had better come back at some later time and put things in order. The mountains would certainly wait for us.

Toward morning we were deep in the fjord. We knew some people in here and thought we might make a call at one of the tiny trading posts. The boat was anchored at a cliff point outside the harbour and I climbed a forested ridge and looked down into the village. A German sentinel was stationed on the dock. We had to go on. We decided to proceed deep into one of the numerous fjord arms, where nature is so wild that there are neither farms nor roads. I knew an old couple who lived there in a lonely cabin, from where it would be possible to get to Sweden. I had been in here once before on a fishing trip.

We found the right arm of the fjord, and the cabin lay there, small and grey, as always, at the foot of the mountain. We paid the skipper and bade him a grateful good-bye.

Yes, the people on the farm had heard that there was war and that the Germans had been evil. The old man would not have believed a word of it if he had not seen it with his own eyes. Once on a fishing trip out in the fjord he had come upon some soldiers in green uniforms. They had fired their guns at him and made a hell of a noise.

We asked him whether he could guide us to Sweden. No, he himself was too old to climb the mountain slopes, but he knew a Laplander boy who knew the way. It was anything, however, but a route for women or children. It would take three days to reach people on the other side of the border, and there were some very treacherous streams to cross. He would fetch the young Laplander, whose name was Leif.

The remainder of the day we rested. We did not say much. Ellen wanted me to get started as quickly as possible. Siri was completely worn out and fell asleep in a chair. When the Laplander arrived we sent him down the

fjord with a message to some friends. We needed food and equipment.
Then we rested again, or we deliberately talked about rather ordinary
things.

Towards evening the boy returned. He brought with him all we had
asked for, and much more. There was a message also. Our friends advised
me to go immediately. My name had been broadcast together with those
of other Norwegians whom the Germans wanted detained. I need not
fear, my friends said, they would take good care of my family.

The message made the decision for us, even though we had known that
this would be the only way out. The knapsack was packed, with Job's
coat on top. Leif carried a bag. We made hasty farewells and started the
mountain climb.

It was a beautiful night, the weather clear and chilly, but I was tired
and our progress was not fast. At intervals we made bonfires of heather
and dwarf-birch. We tried to get snatches of sleep while the heat lasted,
and then were on our way again. Leif was eighteen years old, but he had
been twice to the Lofot fisheries. He was thin and sinewy, almost too good
a marching companion. His father owned a farm with four cows. It must
be his mother who was a Laplander, I thought. We kept up a little conversation to begin with; but, later, we just marched on and on in silence.

The next morning after ten hours of walking and climbing we reached
the cairn marking the Swedish border.

Yes, the years had passed quickly, although much had happened. The
time ahead might not move so rapidly.

Wearily I rose and adjusted my knapsack. I prized Job's coat, but my
pleasure in possessing it did not lessen its weight. We continued our march
into Sweden.

After two days of tramping we arrived at the first Swedish Laplander
colony. These were real Laplanders with tents and reindeer. They were
friendly and helpful, and directed us to a tourist cabin where Swedish
relief organizations had deposited blankets and food stores with the order
that no money was to be asked of refugees from Norway. The log cabin
was large and comfortable. We met a dozen Norwegians who had already
made their escape. Most of them had been soldiers. One had brought his
sweetheart along. She cooked our meals and he was very proud. He had
oiled his gun with fat and buried it behind the barn at home, he said. He
might have need for it.

The following day we were taken to the nearest military post. The
Norwegian soldiers had to be temporarily interned, but the others were
permitted to proceed. I went to Stockholm.

A strange atmosphere permeated the Swedish capital. The city was just the same as before, except that the cars had small wood-burning stoves in the rear for fuel. The newspapers wrote about neutrality and "gengas," the new wood-gas car fuel. There were soldiers and officers in all the streets and Germans in the hotels. In the lobby of the Grand Hotel I saw Dr. Kant pounding the hotel desk and demanding his mail. One of the hotel employees said he was a well-known German business man with connections everywhere.

I had heard that Mrs. J. Borden Harriman, the American Minister to Norway, had arrived in Stockholm, and I met her at the Grand. Ever since she had come to Norway as American Minister in 1937 she had been known as one of our country's great foreign friends. I thought she might assist me in securing a visa to the United States. I was not disappointed.

It was not easy to travel across the world in wartime and preparations for the start seemed to take an eternity.

There were many Norwegians in Stockholm burning with a desire to get back to work. Some were officers and soldiers who had been through the fighting, others were officials and workers who had refused to work under German tyranny.

We learned the details of the battles in southern Norway. There had been furious fighting, and the Germans had lost sixty thousand men. British assistance had been sadly inadequate; only territorials had been sent. Often the men did not know how to handle the machine guns, and the young officers had been forced to take over. Behind each destroyed machine-gun nest there had been dead British officers. They had done their best.

We were received with the greatest friendliness by the Swedes. Before the war we had never felt any differences between our neighbours and ourselves. We had shared the same views and the same illusions. The old illusions we had lost and in their stead we had gained a new world-view that was, perhaps, both more or less than illusion. The war was not over, even though the whole of Europe seemed to be under Nazi domination. We believed in the coming victory over German tyranny, but we felt something besides. We had an inner certainty that, before the victory was won, the tidal wave would continue to rise, and that it would spread throughout the world. In the shadows cast by our burning cities we had divined the dark truth, unclear and terrifying, that not one country or one home would be spared. Yet, half-unconsciously, too, we understood that the day of reckoning would come. So great was the injustice that the whole of humanity would rise against it, or be obliged to bow its head and build new temples for it on the ruins of the old.

Through our legation in Stockholm we received word from our Government in London. Its attitude was the same as ours: everything or nothing! No way led back to Norway but the way of victory. Our states-

men and our seamen had saved our merchant fleet, and it was now in the
fight on the side of Great Britain. Our gold reserves had been carried over
the mountains through the bombing attacks to the west coat. From there
it had gone on fishing vessels north to Tromsö and thence abroad. Every
ounce had come out. Yes, we believed in victory, in victory not only for
our way of life, and in eventual liberty and peace, but in military victory
for our weapons, the weapons which, as yet, we did not have.

Our calm Swedish friends told us that they loved us but that we were
mad. Somewhat mad, we from the other side of the Kjölen Mountains
had, perhaps, always been, but now, they said, we were war psychopaths.
We had been taken by surprise from our bed and thrown into ice water,
and it had been too much for us.

Perhaps we were out of our minds, yet the world itself did not seem
very sane, and our experience had been of our world, the world of reality.
Of course, we might have had to admit that, if it had been Sweden and
not us that had been lying on the outside of that Scandinavian double bed,
if it had been Sweden and not us that had been thrown out of it, we, too,
perhaps, might still be neutral, even though we had always shown a greater
tendency to madness.

Again it was the inactivity that was the worst. One did not know what
to do. Then I met an old friend from Oslo. We talked under such circumstances that our conversation made a strong impression upon me. He had
been one of the leaders in intellectual circles in Norway, after having lived
twenty years in America. His rich experience, his radical views, and his
strong personality had placed their imprint upon all the young students
who had come under his influence. In earlier years his opinions and guid-
ance had been an important factor in the shaping of my life. Now he lay
on his deathbed in Stockholm, ill of a brain disease. He had gone to
Sweden for an operation just before the invasion. He advised me to go
to America. In his opinion the United States would become the deciding
power in this revolutionary era.

Other refugees from Norway told us that the civilian population was
beginning to recover after the initial shock, that some people still believed
that the Germans would act like civilized human beings, and that there
were very few quislings.

From Norway came news of an organized underground movement.
At first, it had been largely in the form of small, isolated groups which
hid away weapons and smuggled out information and refugees. Now there
were growing signs that an intensified active resistance was being organized
to combat the German attempt to nazify the country.

Through the underground I managed to get word to Ellen that I had
an opportunity to go to the United States.

XVI

Three Soldiers

BEFORE leaving Stockholm, I spent a whole night talking with three Norwegian boys in a small hotel room. They were very young, and all had served in the war in Norway. Two were students from the University of Oslo, one of them a small law student wearing heavy glasses, the other a tall, handsome medical student. The third was a fairhaired, stocky peasant boy from the coast north of Trondheim.

We chanced to meet in a restaurant and, later, walked together after a Norwegian meeting at which a member of our Government had spoken. I invited them to my room for a smoke and a glass of beer. We all felt a need for unburdening our minds.

I told them that I was on my way to America to enlist the aid of our kinsmen there in our cause, to report what had happened in Norway, and to tell them that, although we had been temporarily defeated, the fight would go on and that they need not be ashamed of the homeland.

The small student in glasses laughed bitterly.

"I'm afraid you cannot use me as an example," he said. He looked searchingly at each of us. "I am utterly and completely ashamed. I have not been able to talk with anyone about my experience, but I can think of nothing else. Perhaps it would help if I talked about it."

We urged him to go ahead.

"Well," he went on, "I enlisted on the first day and was a soldier as long as it lasted. I didn't see any front-line fighting except on one occasion—and then I failed miserably."

There was a long pause before he continued. He forced himself to go on.

"During the retreat through the valley south of Dovre I volunteered on a special squad that was charged with holding a curve on the road until

our troops could take positions farther up the valley. We must hold it for
only one hour, but during that time no one must be allowed to get
through. There were four of us, three privates and a lieutenant. He had a
strong, tanned face, and I remember that he had lost his cap. We blocked
the road with logs and then took cover above the highway. I mentioned
the fact that I had competed in some shooting meets and was put in a front
position. The rest lay in a slanting line above. The Lieutenant stood behind
a pine tree between me and the next man, field glasses to his eyes.

"We were there for only a few minutes when we heard motor-cycles
coming up from below. The Lieutenant reported that he saw three of
them. They were Germans, apparently on a reconnaissance trip. None
must be permitted to return. The entire value of our mission depended
upon that. We must take accurate aim. He would give the order to fire.

"When the Germans discovered the barricade they slowed up. One of
them stopped directly below me. He half turned his motor-cycle. I had
him at dead aim all the time. The other two rode slowly toward the
barricade, and looked anxiously around. The first one must have seen us.
He shouted a warning. My man threw himself into the ditch only a few
yards below me.

" 'Fire!' the Lieutenant shouted.

"Shots went off all along the line. Both the Germans on the highway
dropped dead. I touched the trigger but could not make myself press it.
It was the first time I was shooting at a human being. He lay with his
back toward me and had absolutely no chance.

" 'Hi!' I shouted, to give him an opportunity to turn and reach for his
gun. He rolled over and remained seated on the shoulder of the road. When
he saw me he raised his hands above his head. I bobbed my gun up and
down to indicate he was to rise and come forward. He nodded, but, as
he rose, he let one hand down, as though to steady himself. Instead, he
reached for a hand grenade in his belt and when his hand went up again
it let go an oblong object which came whistling toward us. It exploded
right behind me. I heard a moan. It was our Lieutenant. His lower bowel
had been ripped out. I saw blood and intestines streaming out as he leaned
against the tree. From the road I heard the motor-cycle starting up. My
glasses were knocked off by the explosion. When I got them on again the
German was out of range.

"I crawled up to the pine tree. The Lieutenant lay with his head against
the trunk. I knelt beside him and placed my jacket over his torn stomach.
He lifted his hand and touched me. It was like a caress.

" 'You are a good fellow,' he whispered hoarsely, 'but you are no good
in a war.' His face was drawn in terrible agony. The others came out and
wanted to carry him back to the main force. There was an ambulance

there. But the Lieutenant managed to whisper that we must hold the position for the full hour. From my place next to the stone I could see his face, ashen beneath the tan. He made an almost imperceptible sign with his head that I must keep my eyes forward. When I looked at him again his head had fallen to the side.

"We lay there an eternity and nothing more happened. At the end of the hour he was dead. We carried him on our guns through the woods.

"I was never sent back into the fighting. I was no good!

"The next week southern Norway was given up. I was near the Swedish border when our company was demobilized and I came across the border with some other boys. I have reported for service every day at the Norwegian office in Stockholm. There must be something I can do! I have not sent word home that I am still alive. I will never have peace but I must find a way to remove that blot, to prove that I am good for something."

Silence followed his story.

"You needn't feel ashamed," I finally said. "You were just like the rest of our nation. We are not adjusted to killing. We are a civilized people."

He shook his head and gave us a hopeless stare from behind his heavy glasses.

"It makes no difference what you call it. We lost our country because there were too many like me. It was men like the Lieutenant that we needed, not bookworms in glasses."

"You'll get your chance, you may be sure of that," the tall student interrupted. "We'll all be in it again. I, too, was through the whole affair. We fired incessantly, but still we had to withdraw. There was certainly no lack of will to fight, but, so far as I was concerned, I never felt that the enemy was anything personal. We just fired at those green uniforms as long as we could.

"It didn't become personal until it was all over. Details of the battles I don't recall, but I shall never forget one incident that occurred after the fighting was over. The communication line had been broken. We were without ammunition all day. In the evening we were told that we would have to surrender at dawn. I got some civilian clothing and escaped through the German lines. I, too, wanted to get to Sweden. I did not like the idea of surrendering, not least, perhaps, because I could not stand the thought of standing defeated before those arrogant Germans.

"The night before I crossed the border I walked alone through a dense forest. The moon was up and the forest was calm, except for a slight stir in the treetops. Suddenly I smelled a strange odour. It reminded me of the frying odour from the student restaurant. I used to have my seat in the corner of the great Reading Room. You remember it opens toward the side of the building over the University kitchen.

"Then I saw the reflection of a fire between the trees. Soon I came to a clearing in the forest and there, in an open field, a little homestead was blazing. I did not see any human being about, but the odour of burning flesh was strong.

"I climbed a fence and approached the place. A little log cabin and an old barn were being destroyed by an intense, smokeless fire. Then I discovered that there was a human being there. In the farmyard next to the pump an old peasant woman sat. A steel helmet and a can lay beside her. She had apparently tried to extinguish the fire but had given it up. Now she sat motionless with parted legs on the bare ground. Her face was blank and expressionless. I tried to talk to her. I told her she must not sit there like that. Her clothes might catch fire. She gave me no answer, but straightened her skirt with a thin, worn hand.

"I carried a can of water to the burning buildings, but they were beyond salvage. Then I discovered what was causing the odour. The buildings were full of German corpses. Some still had steel helmets on. They were glowing red. Some of the faces seemed to be grinning sardonically through the flames.

"I went back to the old woman and poured some of the water over her. It seemed to help. A faint expression came over her face, some of the blankness went out of the stare. 'Lord Jesus, Lord Jesus,' she moaned. I helped her to her feet and steadied her into the field below the house. She tottered a bit, but kept her balance, and talked a little.

"She had lived on the farm with her two sons. When they heard about the war, they caught a bus going south down the valley, and she had not heard anything more of them. She had been alone right up to the day before yesterday, when some Norwegian soldiers had happened by. They had warned her that there would be shooting and that she had better move up into the mountains. She felt, however, that she was too old to flee to the woods, so she had just turned the cattle out. Yesterday there had been shooting all over the valley, but she had not seen any soldiers until late in the evening. Then some German soldiers had arrived with truckloads of corpses and had piled the dead men into the cabin and in the hay in the barn and set them afire. She had tried to put out the fire, and, when they held her back she splashed water on the soldiers. They had just laughed at her and taken a helmet that had belonged to one of the dead and pressed it down on her head, so that she could not see anything. When the houses were well on fire, the soldiers disappeared.

"I tried to get the woman to come along with me, but she asked where she could go. Then I had to leave her to make my own escape through the forest.

"It was not much of an incident, perhaps. The Germans had destroyed city after city. They had burned and looted the whole countryside. But this poor little farm made into a hideous funeral pyre and this hopelessly homeless old woman somehow awakened me. It suddenly became a personal necessity to get back to those woods and fight again. I don't know whether you understand what I mean, but that is the way I feel."

"I understand perfectly, and I feel the same way," said the heavy-set blond boy from Trindelag.

His broad dialect filled the little room. We had no lights, but an advertising sign on the roof outside threw great splashes of light through the window. He lowered his voice as he continued.

"I was called to the colours at New Year. We participated in manœuvres, first up in northern Norway, and, later, down by Trondheimsfjord. In the beginning of the war I took part in the fighting there. We met disaster from the start. The English came to Namsos. Their weapons were not much better than ours. There seemed to be no order to anything, and we doubted whether our officers had any real plans at all. The boys wanted to counter attack and retake Trondheim. The officers said we were not strong enough, we must wait for the British. But the British did not manage to hold even Steinkjær at the foot of the fjord. More and more Germans were shipped in. They kept the fjord the whole time and they dominated the air. Whatever we tried amounted to nothing. They destroyed all the cities we held down there. Steinkjær was blown to bits from the sea and Namsos was bombed from the air. I saw both cities burn to the ground. I drove through Steinkjær just as the church was burning. I and my six brothers had all been baptized and confirmed in that church.

"I had a motor-cycle and was serving as a messenger. It was plain hell. I was thus prevented from taking part in any of the fights, but in compensation I had the cycle and escaped towards the north when the British had evacuated and the fighting was off in that section. I took part in all the fighting throughout the Northland. I left the cycle on a dock at Mosjöen and shipped on board a fishing boat for Bodö. I remember it was May 23rd. That was the day they annihilated that town. The German planes began with the hospital and then destroyed the rest of the city. I went north again to fight, but I had no hope of victory.

"We had some wonderful days in the mountains north of Narvik. We shot Germans like rabbits and took one snow-peaked mountain after another. But, inside, I knew it was all in vain. We could never win.

"But finally I had my experience too. A small thing, perhaps, but it changed my whole view. It happened the day we had to give up. I was at Sætermoen when General Ruge returned from his arbitrations with the Germans. The boys said that he had tried to keep the northernmost part of the country free. He had the respect of the Germans, they said. Everybody must respect General Ruge. We soldiers loved him. I did not believe that the Germans would offer us any concessions. They would grab our land as well as all the rest of the world. We could only hope that the next generation might, perhaps become brutalized enough to beat them.

"The General returned with just the message I had expected. We must surrender unconditionally.

"We stood on the old parade grounds for a last parade. We were going to be demobilized. The Germans would come the same evening to take over. We would be sent either to prison camps or back to our homes to work as slaves on our own farms.

"A hush settled over the grounds when the General appeared. We had not said much before, but now we were all breathlessly silent. His words were brief and definite, like a command, but they were also like a personal greeting and a friendly farewell to each one of us.

"He said that we could not fight any more for the time being, but that the war was not over. We would never be free merely by waiting for help from the outside. We were going to fight again. He implored us to remain faithful and to be ready for that day. He paused for an instant and a twitch crossed his fine face. I remember he said, 'Whether I am dead or alive I will be with you on that day.'

"I could not look at him any more, or I would have sobbed aloud. I tried to think of something else. I stood on the extreme end next to the fence towards the highway. Across the road a young girl was standing. She lived on a farm not far from our camp. Every morning she had come with a wheelbarrow filled with milk cans. I had helped her a few times but I had never talked with her and did not know her name. I had thought of her often and called her Solveig to myself. She saw that I was looking at her. She was sobbing and made no attempt to hide it, but there was a strange glow on her face and she smiled as if she wished to share her faith with me. I glanced at the officers, who stood stiffly erect behind the little General, and I looked along the rows of boys. All the faces were shining. And then I knew that we were going to succeed, anyhow. The men and the women were what really counted. The tools we could get. Life suddenly became very simple. We would do what the General said. We would be faithful and ready. We would not just wait. We were going to liberate ourselves! Our children would not have to do it. I would flee abroad and learn something, so that I might be ready for that day. Afterwards I would return to this very place. I knew of a sheltered spot in the valley that could be cleared. I would build a home there with Solveig. Our children would live there."

He smiled.

"Well, fellows, you know how one may dream of silly things when your heart is so full that it hurts. Anyway, I managed to escape to the mountains before the Germans marched in. I carried my gun until I had to surrender it to the Swedish border guard. I told him to keep it oiled so that it would not be rusty when I came back for it. He laughed and said it might well be that we would be fighting side by side on that day.

"I was kept in an internment camp for a while in northern Sweden, but a few days ago I got permission to come to Stockholm. I said I had a kind of aunt here. Now they tell me that our Government is planning an air training school in Canada. To-day I talked with some Norwegian officers, and they promised to send me over as soon as plans are a little further along.

"Defeat is not so bitter, after all, if one does not swallow it. And we are certainly not through with this party yet."

For a while we smoked in silence. We were so tired that we sat for a bit before breaking up. The flashes from the sign outside the window came and went with steady regularity, lighting up the young faces. It was almost morning. We said that we would meet again in Norway, but that we would return as other men. The change that we felt in process in us was, perhaps, only a beginning. The war would recreate us in its own image. How hard and brutal and unmindful of life and feeling had we to become before we could take our country back again? Perhaps it was just as well that we did not know the price, but we said that no matter how high it should be we would pay it. We got up and gave one another our hands in farewell, and each handshake was a promise.

XVII

Long Journey

A T last I had passport and visa and money and ticket. There was no other connection between Sweden and Russia than the air route from Stockholm to Moscow, but the best was good enough. There were ten of us in the plane, half of us Scandinavian, the rest Englishmen travelling the wrong way to get back home.

We left Stockholm early in the morning and arrived at Riga about noon. Russia had occupied the Baltic states a few days earlier. In Esthonia things looked quiet, but the stop was short and we had neither time nor opportunity to see very much. In the evening we landed at the Dynamo Airfield in Moscow.

Our tickets were paid in advance, with hotel accommodations and meal tickets. A sombre seriousness lay over the Red capital. We had to wait more than a week for room on the Siberia Express. The official tourist bureau "Intourist" took care of us. We were well treated, but it did not appear that Moscow was greatly interested in furthering the tourist trade. The visit to Russia was not a holiday trip but we felt considerably more secure.

Fifteen years earlier I had been in Moscow as a young student. Even at that time there had not been much comfort, but there had been more interest and fascination. There had been flying banners and optimism. A new and fuller way of life was just around the corner. There had been mass meetings with posters and songs. Now Moscow was characterized by a peculiar grey resoluteness. Soldiers filled the streets. Their equipment was excellent and they were better dressed than the common people, but they did not sing. It was as if they were preparing for a threatening danger without knowing from what corner it would strike. Now the imperative problems were machines and weapons, not principles and world revolution. The only land whose name had a good sound was the United States of America. But even in Moscow there were Germans in all the hotels.

Our meal tickets were issued for only a brief stay, but there was a demand for clothing, and by selling a topcoat and a swimming suit we got ample funds for our needs. In the stores there was nothing to be had except food and vodka.

The week after our arrival we were packed into the Siberia Express. It was a fast train, but the trip took nine days. The diner had an atmosphere of long-lost glory with tasselled curtains and waiters who asked whether we wanted chicken or fish, fruit or ice. The individual orders were carefully written up, whereupon we all got beef stew and pudding.

The days were long and dirty. We played cards or chess with one another and with Russian officers, who were friendly but indifferent. They refused to discuss politics, but wanted to buy our wrist watches.

Siberia looked better than its reputation. We could see few highways, but many airfields. Finally we traversed the seemingly endless continent and once more could see the ocean.

We knew that Vladivostok was a much sought-after city, but it was not apparent why. There was work in the vicinity and many projects seemed to be going forward, but there was neither joy nor enthusiasm. In Vladivostok we had to wait again. Here, too, the hotel was filled, but only with bedbugs; there were no Germans.

The Intourist representative who had accompanied us throughout the journey, and who functioned as interpreter, uncle, and propagandist, regretted that our trip through Soviet Russia had not been more comfortable. He said, however, that we would not find it any better on the Japanese steamer to Tsuruga. Uncle Intourist was not lying. At our parting he declined a tip with indignation, but accepted as a personal remembrance a suit of Swedish BVD's, and a safety razor.

It took us three days to reach Japan in a freighter that sailed down the Korean coast. We went on to Tokyo and Yokohama and there the travelling party was dissolved. It was difficult to get on. The steamers were overloaded. A hectic life pulsated everywhere in Japan. There was far more merchandise in the stores than there had been in Russia, but most of it was substitute for something else. Once again we were to find Germans in the hotels.

If it had been difficult to grasp the Russian attitude, it was not going to be any easier to understand the Japanese. It was said in the consulates that, among the common people, whose standard of living was steadily on the decline, the war had long since lost its popularity. Year after year they had been sending their sons to China and had got nothing in return

except victory bulletins and small white boxes, the latter presumably containing the ashes of the heroes. It was strictly forbidden, under threat of
both temporal and eternal punishment, to open these boxes, but the whisper went from man to man that they contained nothing but sand from
the beaches of Shanghai.

The newspapers dispensed the queerest forms of propaganda. The *Japan
Advertiser* published a call to celebrate the Day of the Rabbits, "in the
honour of these humble creatures that are giving their skins for the army
and the fatherland and in that manner setting an example for the rest of
us." In the streets young fanatics raved into loud-speakers against the alien
civilization and the white devils.

Everywhere there was a strange mixture of mysticism and common
sense. Workers clattered through the streets on wooden sandals to ultra-
modern workshops and factories. The women kept humbly three feet
behind their husbands. They were dressed in their beautiful long kimonos
bound with the insanely impractical stomach belts made up of yards and
yards of stiff silk, but they visited up-to-date sports arenas and went
swimming without swimming suits in public mixed pools. The food
seemed to come from laboratories rather than from primitive oriental
kitchens. The most modern airplanes were equipped with the latest automatic safety devices and were decorated with symbols to keep evil spirits
away. No, it certainly was not easy to understand the soul of modern
Japan, which might also prove itself to be a substitute.

After I had waited for three weeks, a Norwegian cargo liner arrived,
on which I was able to book passage for Los Angeles. I was again on
Norwegian ground. The ship had been at sea on April 9th. Confusing
and contradictory orders had come through the radio. From Oslo there
had been instructions to return home at once. From London and Stockholm came the call of the Nygårdsvold Cabinet to proceed to Allied or
neutral harbours. Like all other Norwegian seamen, the officers and sailors
on board had placed themselves at the disposal of the Norwegian Government. Scarcely any of them had heard from their families in Norway
since the day of invasion.

The Pacific lived up to its name. We had a peaceful voyage.

Los Angeles, San Francisco—America! Perhaps, after all, it was not too
different from the mental picture I had already formed of it. The super-
abundance and the wastefulness, the noise and the traffic, the sea of lights
at night, the frightening dimensions of everything—to a certain extent
I found it depressing. I examined my heart. It was not envy, it was rather
anxiety and fear, that all this practical wealth and all these tough-minded
and busy people would refuse to believe in ghosts. It was not that one
was not met by friendliness and personal good will; of these things there

was almost too much. But how could one ever expect that this self-sustaining and self-sure continent would come to look upon that one insane military state in Central Europe as a threat to all free peoples everywhere?

I went north to Seattle and east from there, through the country where Norwegian immigrants had settled. The feeling was the same as it had been on the coast. Their reaction was one of compassion.

It was a pity that the war had engulfed us!

And yet, I realized that, not so long ago, we, too, had held that view, exactly that view, so far as other countries were concerned. What could we expect of this great nation, where there was such an abundance of liberty and consumable goods and where the possibilities still seemed limitless?

This was Norwegian America. It extended along the coast of the State of Washington, over the mountains into Montana, across the prairies of the Dakotas, to the rich hills of Minnesota, Iowa, and Wisconsin. Everywhere there were Norwegian farmers and craftsmen. They had come here many years ago or their fathers had settled here, because it was too narrow and there was too little soil between the mountains in the homeland. They had found more soil than they had dreamed of, and they had found security. They had become respected citizens with equal rights in great, rich America. And yet they loved Norway, the old Norway, as it stood before them, little, poor, and hard. Pictures of the small grey homesteads they came from hung on the walls, with memories of the Old Country, where poverty, in spite of everything, had had a certain dignity and peace.

Yes, the interest and the sympathy were there. They wanted to help, but they were not willing to risk the one thing they had crossed the ocean to get—security. Many of their forefathers had come in sailing vessels and had told of hazardous voyages. Europe was far, far away.

Some of them asked bluntly, "But you cannot expect us to declare war and send our boys abroad?"

No, we did not expect anything. We could only tell them that we, too, had once held exactly the same opinion. Time would tell whether this was a war for the possession of certain harbours and territories or whether it was a war about oceans and continents and freedom on earth—and time had become immensely precious.

In the history of a nation, a few years, more or less, may, of course, not seem to matter very much. On the other hand, a nation never lives more than a few generations at any given time, and the individual man or woman really ought to have a little something to eat from day to day. Out here in the Middle West, with its thousands of square miles of heavy wheat, it was too easy to talk in terms of generations and to say that the mills of the gods grind slowly.

And yet, it was a fountain of inspiring to meet this Norwegian America these foreign countrymen. They gathered in their stark and sober churches and sat around the coffee cups in the bare church basements to hear about Norway. Their stolid faces were expressive only of work and toil, but their eyes shone. There was power in these faces, and goodness in the clear eyes. They had come to these wild prairies with empty hands, and they had helped to build an Empire. These were the same people we had at home. We would get our country back, more barren and poorer than ever before, but we would rebuild it more beautiful and free than it had ever been.

It was late autumn when I arrived in Washington. I went to the Norwegian Legation, one of the most important centres for free, fighting Norway. There I met Commodore Askim, who, with his wife had come the other way around the world. Again his ship had been torpedoed and sunk; he had been fortunate. It seemed a miracle that our Government and its diplomatic service had succeeded so quickly in building a new Government apparatus outside the country, and in securing such accurate and detailed information through the newly-organized Information Service. Not all the news was good. The country was being looted. The Gestapo *was* very busy, attempting to nazify the people.

The temporary administrative Council in Oslo had been painstakingly re-formed with Quisling's men. All the former political parties had been declared illegal except for Quisling's infinitesimal and insignificant group.

The civic administrations of the various localities were being liquidated as rapidly as sufficient numbers of traitors could be found. In Narvik, a railway telegraph operator named Trældal had been "appointed" mayor. Trældal had always had Nazi sympathies, a view shared only by Sundlo, and had been shunned or ridiculed by the people.

The prisons were crowded and concentration camps had been built and were being used. Hundreds of our best people were in them.

Personally, I received bad news. Ellen had been taken by the Gestapo. She was not imprisoned, but was kept under surveillance.

Strangely, radios had not, as yet, been confiscated. The Germans evidently still thought it possible to win the people with their propaganda. It was, of course, forbidden to listen to foreign stations, but now the whole nation was made up of lawbreakers. We could still talk with Norway.

The stream of youth that fled in boats and across the mountains continued to grow. We heard that the underground was well organized and was functioning smoothly and well. The Home Front was no longer led by amateurs. The lessons of the New Order had been quickly learned. The newspapers told of avalanches in the mountains. Highways and railroads were being washed out. Even the mountains were growing impatient.

XVIII *Norway Sails On*

E VEN while the fighting was raging in Norway the huge Norwegian merchant marine was conscripted to serve under a special commission appointed by the Government. Thus the Norwegian Shipping and Trade Mission, *Nortraship*, became the largest shipping organization in the world. A new administration was quickly set up, with major offices in London, Montreal, and New York. Approximately twenty-five thousand seamen and one thousand ships were thrown into the battle of transport and the race for time.

The New York office was completely organized and functioning smoothly when I called in December, 1940. The office was a scene of intense activity, and, despite the fact that the force comprised more than one hundred officials and office workers, there was a shortage of technical help. Our ships, most of them modern, sailed all the seven seas. They had been our pride, and represented a large share of our wealth; they had given to our relatively poor nation the necessary income for maintaining our high living standard and our culture. The Norwegian merchant marine was built for peaceful competition in world trade; but, whenever the freedom of the seas had been challenged, our ships had been of vital importance. The first World War had cost Norway more than half of her pre-war tonnage, a loss greater than that of any of the belligerent nations. Now, with our country conquered and occupied by the enemy, it was our merchant marine that gave us a position which counted among our Allies. The course was so precarious, the danger so great, that only realities mattered. Two hundred and seventy-two fast oil tankers was a contribution that did count. I looked at the charts and at pictures of our finest ships, many of them already marked with black crosses.

I met seamen waiting to make the next trip across the treacherous Atlantic. One evening a group of us chanced to meet and sit together in a restaurant on the Battery. It was not the best place in the world for conversation. Sailors with too many loose coins kept the music box working overtime. This nuisance was a huge monster of a thing, shrill both in sound and colour. I thought it must have some kind of internal fountain that pumped coloured water through glass tubes. It was not exactly the kind of thing that made foreigners love America.

The boys preferred not to talk of their torpedo sinkings. When, once in a while, they did have a peaceful night ashore, they said, why spoil it?

"But I do remember one funny thing," a stocky bos'n said. He smiled over his glass of beer. "We had been in a life boat for five days, three days without water. The U-boat had machine-gunned us and had riddled the water tank and destroyed the motor. We rowed until we were exhausted and after that we drifted. Someone began to talk about beer in great round barrels; light, fresh beer that bubbled with fine pearls coming up from the bottom. Someone else said we had better get a taxi and be on our way; perhaps there were some new regulations on closing hours; one could never tell with a war on. We begged him to shut up. But after a while we were all agreed that the most sensible thing to do was to call the taxi and get something to eat and drink. We actually imagined that the taxi stood waiting for us, with the taximeter humming. That was funny!"

"And then?"

"Well, that was all that was funny about it."

"And then you were saved?"

"No, not until the next day. We were picked up by a British destroyer, but not before three of the fellows had jumped overboard to—the taxi. I might have jumped myself, but the machinist's mate hit me on the head with the baler. That really helped the thirst. He always had been a teetotaller. Fine fellow, though. He was torpedoed during the last war, too.

"We go out again to-morrow. What do you think of the situation in Norway? Whenever I sit down to bacon and eggs in the mess room and think of those at home, the food chokes me."

We talked of the Home Front. We resented the fact that some newspapers had referred to it as passive resistance. Except for the lack of weapons, the resistance itself was certainly active enough. Quisling and the Germans had liquidated all the old political parties; youth and sports organizations had been taken over; but the New Order was meeting sabotage and resistance from all sides. The prisons were already filled with good Norwegians. At that, it appeared that the nazification was in its relatively innocent beginnings. We had reports that constantly new

The Mountains Wait

172

groups of the Gestapo were coming into the country. The Trade Union
was likely to be hit next. Earlier in the autumn, decrees had prohibited
workers engaged in agriculture, lumbering, fishing, and shipping from
changing jobs or moving from the country into the towns. The food
situation was becoming steadily worse. Sooner or later there would be
starvation.

"*We* can certainly take it," said the bos'n when we rose to go, "but
what we fear is that we will have to go to the graveyards to find our
families when we go home."

That attitude prevails among all Norwegian seamen. They are harder
and tougher than landsmen, but they are also more emotional and sen-
timental. The heavy, monotonous routine, broken by moments of high
excitement and utmost danger, makes for a strange dualism. The long and
lonely watches filled with daydreams and anxiety for those at home, the
U-boat psychosis, and the horrors in the life boats, combine to produce
a special, peculiar reaction. The sailors do their work, not consciously
realizing the unequal burden the war has placed upon them; but, on the
other hand, the distress and want of those at home press even stronger
on their nerves. To us ashore there seems to be abundant time for preparation, but to those on ships there is always need for haste. They bring the
rich, heavy cargoes to England and other of our Allies, but never any
food to the homeland. The morale of the sailors is largely a question of
understanding their problem. But perhaps it is a question, too, of whether
we on land can measure up to them.

I was invited to return to the Middle West, and visited all the more
important Norwegian centres as well as filling many lecture engagements.
Our kinsmen seemed to feel a little less pity for us now and a little more
anxiety on their own behalf. Still, the feeling that they were spectators at
a seemingly unexplainable accident persisted.

Dramatization of the fact that their old Norway had been brought into
the focus of world-wide attention was often a little too dominant. Many
times I was to meet with such statements as, "You probably saw me at
your lecture last night. I have an aunt in Bodö. Of course the Germans
have shot her by now." When I offered the consolation that not too many
civilians had been shot, the reaction was often one of wounded pride. Of
course the aunt had been shot!

On the whole, however, the feeling of sympathy and a desire to help
was stronger and more frequent than the dramatization of the sensational.
The relationship between the emigrants and those at home had always
been close, and, like the gulf stream, the material benefits of the connection
seemed always to have moved in one direction. With "America money"
many families in Norway had built that new home or repaired the old.

Immediately after the invasion, committees for Norwegian Relief were organized throughout the United States. The collection of funds and materials was limited only by the difficulties of sending them abroad.

In spite of its isolation, however, news—the real news—came in a steady stream from Norway, and there were, occasionally, letters. They had been opened and censored, but at least they were signs of life.

Ellen and I, on our excursion through the fjords, had talked of ways we might keep in touch with each other if we could not write letters directly. We made up a code based on memories we shared. I was to be a sailor with a large family. We created aunts and uncles all over Norway and they happened to live in rather important places. Crabbed old Uncle Eric was Gestapo. As was natural, he became more and more disagreeable and suspicious in his old age, and tolerated no liberty for the young.

It worked. None of this family detail was blacked out by the censors, and for a while I got a fairly clear idea of what was happening. Then the letters stopped, although other mail was still coming through. I feared the worst but hoped for the best.

I received greetings from friends in London and letters from my father. Things were taking shape. To move around had never been his greatest pleasure and certainly working conditions were not the best for an elderly gentleman. He had always taken life as it came, and now it was coming fast and furiously. During the worst period of the bombing of London Norway had set up a new Government organization.

I lectured all the winter. In February, 1941, at Sioux Falls, South Dakota, I received a forwarded cable from Stockholm. Ellen and Siri had crossed the border. They would, if possible, be sent through Russia, Siberia, and Japan, and thence to the United States. I read avidly everything I could lay my hands on concerning developments in the Far East, and discovered at least one comforting journalist who was of the opinion that the situation there would remain unchanged until the spring.

A month later, when I was in the Eastern states, I received a personal message through our Legation in Tokyo.

We met in Chicago. I thought them both a little pale, but Siri had grown. She had been intensely interested in all the strange things she had seen and experienced. Norway was already far away. She did not remember much about it. But Mother did.

They had lived for some time in the cabin at the base of the mountain in the fjord arm. Then they had returned to Narvik, where they had lived with friends. Many of the workers had been called back and were put to work on the repair or the railway and the docks. The remaining houses were crowded and barracks were being built.

Kittenshill was still intact when they returned, but was occupied by

German "actresses" imported a few weeks after the fighting ceased, to "bolster the morale of the German troops." She had been permitted to take Siri's clothes, but her own were being worn by the ladies. The house had been visited by notables. Reichskommissar Terboven had stayed there when he had been on an inspection tour of Narvik. That was the day that France had capitulated, and neighbours reported that there had been a great celebration in the actresses' house that night.

At first the Germans had paid no attention to her. An officer had even given her a pass. But that had been a trap, for when she attempted to leave the country she had been arrested on the train and returned to Narvik. Her luggage had been ransacked and she had been stripped for inspection.

They questioned her an entire day. Siri caused so many timely interruptions that the Germans finally put her in a soldier's bunk where she fell asleep. As for herself, she didn't know anything. After a few weeks she received permission to go to Oslo, but her movements were watched.

How had she managed with money? I asked.

That had not been so difficult. The Germans had not been much interested in the money of private persons. They continued to print new Norwegian paper money and there was more money in the land than ever before. On the other hand, there was less and less to buy. Even during the first winter there had been almost no meat. Everything was rationed, and it was comparatively simple to get money for the few things that could be had. People in distress were always helped. A kind of freemasonry had sprung up between all loyal Norwegians. No, there were not many quislings. None of our personal friends had gone over to the Nazis.

A strange atmosphere had pervaded Oslo during the first winter. People generally did not know much. Perhaps we over here were somewhat better informed as to what had happened in Norway, but it had been a really great experience to see at first hand how the nation had reacted. It was as though a new kind of social organism was being formed below the surface. Everyone was engaged in secret activity. Illegal groups were at work everywhere. Very few understood the organization of the underground, but it seemed to be the same kind of system that one read of in nineteenth-century Russian novels. Only the key men knew anything about the next floor up in the pyramid. Who was at the top, no one seemed to know.

Hidden radio stations denounced the Germans unendingly and broadcast the names of those who had become traitors. Illegal newspapers carried news as well as the latest jokes about Quisling and Terboven. The Norwegian broadcast from London was a major event of each day.

Ellen had been promised help in leaving the country, but even after she was out she did not know who had arranged the escape. She was told to be ready for instant departure during a certain week. The day was not named. Even her immediate family must not be told of her intention to leave.

One night she and Siri were hurriedly called for. On the trip through the country different means of transportation were used, a new man with each. The last part of the way they had walked. Near the border a boy appeared, and carried Siri through forests into Sweden.

In Stockholm she had met friends. The trip across Russia and Siberia had seemed endless, but, after all, she had only the one child. Other mothers had three and four.

Now the three of us travelled in the Ford. We felt like missionaries, or, at least, were treated as such. We carried a gospel, but were cautious with the commandments. The congregation would have to make its own interpretation and draw its own conclusions.

We had a good but not a peaceful life. Siri, especially, needed more regular hours. We were all happy in the autumn of the year when we received orders to open a Norwegian office in Minneapolis, where a home could once again be established.

One of the first news items the office received for distribution was a brief message stating that Viggo Hansteen had been executed in Oslo. On September 10th he and a young worker, Rolf Vickström, had been condemned to death by a Nazi tribunal. They had been shot the same evening.

Later, we received more details. A strike had been called in certain German-controlled plants in Oslo, and the Germans had declared a state of civil emergency. Covered vanloads of prisoners were driven through the streets all day. Most of the labour leaders who were still free had been arrested, together with hundreds of others who could have had no possible connection with the strike—newspapermen, sports leaders, teachers, business men. Even the head of the University of Oslo had been taken.

Orders from the Gestapo came thick and fast. The great Employers' Association was dissolved, as well as such apparently harmless organizations as the Salvation Army, the Boy Scouts, and the Girl Scouts. Groups organized for the sole purpose of reconstructing bombed homes and aiding war-stricken families were ordered to be disbanded.

It was stated in the reports that Hansteen and Vickström were more or less chance victims of the German military court, but Hansteen's friends found it difficult to believe that it had been only accidental that he had been one of the first victims. Why, accidentally, one of the noblest; he, who, in the discussions between the labour organizations and the Reichskommissar, had proved himself so infinitely superior? All those present had made involuntary comparison between this upright, fair, quiet Norse-man, and the raceless, hysterical gangster type that represented the *Herren-volk* in Norway.

A few hours after the death sentence had been passed, the Oslo Radio announced that the executions had already taken place, no one knew where. But, in the concentration camps, where Norwegians, in mysterious ways, were better informed than those outside, the report was tapped out on the walls that the martyrs had been killed by revolver bullets in the neck in the cellar of the Government Building, and that shortly afterwards the clothes of the murdered men had been sent to their families.

We were to receive more and more messages of this nature. During the winter, German attention was turned to the church and schools. The Nazis, working with Quisling, attempted to force passage of new laws affecting public education in Norway looking to complete nazification of our children and our young people. The invaders had already taken everything we owned. Now they wanted to rob us of our greatest treasure, the minds of future Norway. The church leaders and the school authorities took an immediate and absolute stand against what they deemed the worst of all treachery.

The fight between the quislings and the clergy ended in a complete break with the Nazis. The Church of Norway was fighting for the children and was the only church in occupied Europe to voice a fearless condemnation of Hitler's pagan tyranny. The teachers, as one man, protested in indignation, and pledged themselves never to surrender their fidelity to the ideal of free and independent education as guaranteed by the Norwegian Constitution. Teachers by the hundreds were thrown into concentration camps, but neither inhuman brutality nor subtle flattery could break their spirit.

We received information about almost unbelievable acts of terrorism, and heroic resistance that made us proud and humble, ill and happy at the same time.

In the late winter I again went on a lecture tour, this time in Ohio and New York, where I had been asked to speak at several colleges. It was extremely interesting to observe how American students reacted to the problems of war and peace. Again I found the thinking identical with that with which Norway had soothed itself before April 9, 1940—a year and a half before.

After the lectures there were usually discussions, with questions and answers. The students said that they could well understand that we were unprepared, that we had too few weapons, but they could not understand how we could have been taken so completely by surprise.

It was not easy to give a logical and plausible answer, and, at first, my answers were, perhaps, not too convincing. But during the latter part of

Above.—NORWEGIAN SKIING PATROLS DURING TRAINING
IN SCOTLAND

Below.—THE KING OF NORWAY WITH NORWEGIAN
CHILDREN IN SCOTLAND

NORWEGIAN FISHERMEN WHO, HAVING ESCAPED FROM NOR-
WAY ACROSS THE NORTH SEA IN THEIR SMALL BOATS,
BRING REGULAR SUPPLIES TO BRITISH PORTS

the tour it became less difficult. The events of December 7th at Pearl Harbour had occurred in the meantime.

Once more I was to see reactions identically duplicated. When young minds face the necessity of changing their views they change them speedily and ruthlessly. Student convocations had always fascinated me with their inspiring challenge. The young eyes had never been indifferent, but now they glowed with fire. The cause had become their own.

One evening, after a meeting at a college in New York State, I was invited to the president's home for further discussion. Most of the faculty was present. An old professor told me that he thought I had a quite accurate picture of the student mind. The overwhelming majority of students had been more or less passive in their attitude before December 7th. Immediately afterward they all became interventionists. Many of them wanted to discontinue their studies at once, even though they were seniors and about to graduate in a few months. In their impatience they felt that the whole affair might blow over during the Christmas vacation.

The professor asked me whether I was pleased at what had happened, and then quickly begged me not to answer. It was an unfair question, he said. He would answer it himself.

It was a shameful and almost dishonouring blow that America had received between its self-confident eyes, and it had represented a terrible loss of life and material. But he was glad that the war had come to the American people in just that way.

What if Japan had pursued a different course, and had first attacked Russia? America's foresighted President would still have been forced to take action. But would such a step have had the united support of the people? After the declaration had been signed and the casualty lists began to come in, would there not have been questions of doubt as to its necessity? It was not pleasant to be hit first, but the attack had convinced every citizen that America had no other guilt than the same false illusions of peace that had paralysed all other liberty-loving nations.

The kind old professor had seemed to be talking half to himself, as if he needed to formulate his views of this new situation which would dominate the life of his generation. Now he addressed himself directly to me.

"You described in the auditorium to-night what happened in Norway and in Narvik. In one sense, it is the same destiny that has struck all the civilized world. I am an old humanist, and my work will, perhaps, not have any importance for a long time to come. But I cannot but feel that we human beings, first and last, and in spite of everything, are spiritual beings. Those who share the same ideals form one people across all borderlines.

"We have all been taken by surprise by ships which have come out of the fog and blasted our comfortable world to bits. Now our turn, too,

M

has come. From now on it is probably America's war more than that of anyone else. America can lose it, finally and definitely, but America can also win it.

"I suspect that our enemies made very careful studies before they attacked. They have discovered that we are poorly armed. I suppose it must look that way. I am not thinking purely of the military side; I don't know much about that. I am thinking of the young men who must fight this war. Our young people themselves are apparently poorly armed. They are happy, self-centred children of liberty and democracy. They are undisciplined and daring, and they may not know too much about what freedom essentially is, since they have never known anything else.

"But they have what it takes. Discipline and the use of weapons are, after all, only matters of technique. Modern American youth will never give up. Just because they have had so rich a life, we can depend upon them. Together with you of the other nations, we will see this thing through to victory. You may rest assured that Norway will be free again, and that you will go back to rebuild your little town."

In a better humour than I had been in for a long time I travelled west again. The next autumn I returned to the same territory and met some of the same students again. They were not so impatient now. The war was no longer an adventure that would be over soon. This time they really meant business.

On this trip I used the opportunity to go to Canada and visited Toronto where the Royal Norwegian Air Force had built Camp Little Norway.

To the citizens of Toronto it may, perhaps, be only another bothersome military encampment obstructing the view of Lake Ontario; but, to an exiled and homeless Norwegian, it is a glowing symbol that provides a thrilling experience from the moment he glimpses the Norwegian flag flying over the grey barracks. Here are not only office buildings and Government representatives, but schools, workshops, and training fields where Norwegian youth works and learns.

The guide at the entrance stopped me with a challenge in English. From his accent and his face I could tell from just about what section of Norway he had come. He grinned, and said that my accent was not entirely unfamiliar either.

Earnestness and order were the keynotes of the camp. At the time I visited it, it was not yet two years old. It had been established as an emergency measure. Planes Norway had ordered from America before the war had not been finished in time and the men had travelled half-way around the world to learn to fly them. Because America was neutral, the camp was established across the border.

The Norwegian Government in London had done everything in its power to make possible adequate training facilities. Income from the Norwegian merchant marine had provided the necessary funds, as it has for all free Norwegian activities. It was money that had cost lives, and everyone in the camp knew that the best possible use must be made of it. The young fliers themselves wanted to help and taxed their earnings to raise money for new equipment. The plane "Spirit of Little Norway" was purchased from this fund.

Norwegians and friends throughout the western hemisphere came to its aid. A Norwegian plantation owner in Guatemala regularly sent all the coffee the boys could drink. Other Norwegians in South America sent planes. Norwegian-Americans in the United States formed a national organization with headquarters in Minneapolis to provide the little extras that the USO and American homes could give their own sons.

Never have I seen such grown-up young boys.

"Yes, the material is good," the officer said, with ill-concealed pride.

They were all volunteers, and most of them had reached the camp under great difficulty and against heavy odds. Norway lies exactly halfway around the world and those who try to leave face the death penalty if they are caught. Hundreds have already been trained and they continue to come, but no one knows how many have been lost on the way.

We visited the barracks. Discipline was self-administered and military forms seemed to be used only for practical reasons. Orders were so quiet as to be almost inaudible. We had interrupted a singing of the camp's new battle song. The officer said they might continue.

The camp had a new song written by Sigmund Skard, a Norwegian librarian now in Washington, whom the war had made a poet. He had written of the long journeys the boys had made.

"And he certainly had some experience in travelling himself," said the officer. "Last year he came through Siberia with his wife and two sets of twins."

We listened to the song. They were practising the English version so that their Canadian comrades and girl friends might understand it. A light-haired boy sat in an upper bunk and acted as conductor, a toothbrush for a baton. The young voices filled the narrow barracks:

> "Round the wide world, comrades, we have journeyed;
> Birds alone can follow on our trail;
> Now in eagle flocks we come returning;
> Back to Norway like a thundercloud we sail.
> > Norse men! On guard!
> > Norse men! Strike hard!
> Our singing propellers sing best
> > As we storm from the west.

"Unarmed our kinsmen fight on in the homeland;
  Shame to him who fails to do his share;
  Behind a thousand miles of storm-lashed coastline,
  Comrades! They are waiting for us there.
            Norse men! Set forth
            Your course to the North.
  A storm-cloud now foams in the sky
            As we fly.

"Through the night our squadrons drive onward,
  Like the lightning, swift descends our blow.
  In the dawn we see peaks rise above the cloudbanks;
  Norway, free as before, lies below.
            Norse hearts! Be still!
            We know what we will!
  Thy future lies safe in our hand,
            Fatherland!"

More than a thousand boys have come around the earth to this training camp on Lake Ontario. Every one has a daring adventure behind and an adventure not less daring ahead. The chief is a man who seems to have been predestined for exactly this task: equally able in the air, at sports meets, or in ski competitions, and as close to the classic Viking type as a cultured human being can come.

I was interested in meeting recruits who had arrived from Norway recently, but none who had escaped from Norway during the summer had as yet reached Toronto. Experience had shown that their number decreased during the short and light summer nights. One new recruit, however, was expected in a day or two. He had sailed a tiny sailing boat to England a few weeks earlier and had recently arrived in New York on a Norwegian freighter out of London. He had just crossed the border and, at the moment, was waiting for his Canadian visa at Niagara Falls. If I wished to interview him I could find him in one of the hotels there. He was using the name Sverre. He had parents and brothers in Oslo.

On the trip back to the United States I travelled with one of the student pilots. He was waiting for a broken arm to heal and had been given a brief vacation.

We met Sverre in Niagara Falls. With him was a young Norwegian American who had just arrived to volunteer in the Norwegian Air Force. He had recently graduated from a college in Minnesota and wished to see Niagara Falls before going on to Toronto. We all went sightseeing. Sverre confided his disappointment. There was too much water and too little fall to suit his Norwegian taste.

When we had paid proper attention to the falls, we returned to the hotel for a chat. The newspapers contained reports of the raid at Dieppe in which Commandos and airmen from many of the United Nations had participated. The student pilot related how the Norwegian flyers had distinguished themselves during that historic raid. He had already lost several friends over France, but he did not know what the Norwegian losses had been this time.

We listened to the news over the radio. It was bad, as usual. The Russians were making a desperate stand in the outskirts of Stalingrad. Their irresistible will to struggle and sacrifice made us all humble. It seemed to be the rule with this amazing, distant, fighting people, that their actions caused either offence and indignation or unbounded admiration. What could we not learn from their great faith and their unyielding will! They were fighting hard, and alone. The great armies in the British Isles lay idle. What had become of the Second Front?

The student pilot said that he had feared all the summer that the Second Front would be opened before he had his wings, and, when he had broken his arm during an emergency landing, he had been completely sunk. He might as well have saved himself the despair, he said, for it did not appear that the Second Front would become a reality any time during the year. What were the Generals waiting for?

The college student ventured the opinion that they were wrangling and playing politics just like politicians everywhere. He asked us to speak English since he could not understand or use the Norwegian expression that fitted the occasion. He had learned his Norwegian from his grandmother.

We asked Sverre what he thought and what the people in Norway were thinking. Were they impatient?

He was the youngest in the party, and somewhat bashful. First he tried to use his school English, but quickly dropped into Norwegian. He warmed to his subject and told us with eagerness how things had developed after the Germans had crushed the armed resistance. Impressions and incidents streamed from him in a topsy-turvy flow, almost as if he had forgotten that he had an audience. As his story poured forth his youthful face, resting in cupped hands supported by elbows on the table, became alive with character and maturity.

He related small humiliating incidents which carried pestilence into the grey everyday life at home; of the endless lines before the food stores where women and children stamped their feet to keep them warm in worn-out footwear; of German officers who whizzed through the streets in their commandeered cars, spattering bystanders with mud; and of their wives who sailed by the waiting lines and went directly to the specialty counters reserved for the superior race.

He told of the shocks that came at intervals when islands and villages were devastated in revenge for some minor incident, or new lists of respected Norwegian names were posted as "condemned for illegal and treacherous activities." He told stories of terror and torture that had found their way through prison walls. One's gorge rose in powerless indignation.

Yes, they *were* becoming impatient at home, but he brought to us the message that they could take it!

In a manner, also, he could bring us greetings from the land itself. He had walked across all southern Norway to escape. He was one of the four young men who had planned to make their get-away by sailing a small boat hidden in a fjord on the west coast. They were all from Oslo, but they had travelled alone to avert suspicion. And yet it had been evident that the people on all the farms where he had spent the nights seemed to understand. They had not said as much, but they had been exceptionally cordial and solemn when they bade farewell and asked him to take greetings where he was going. It had been the most beautiful hike he had ever made.

When he arrived at the western fjord, two of his companions were already there, but the third failed to arrive. They waited for several days; but, finally, had to set sail, since the moon was growing brighter.

In England, the other two had enlisted in the Royal Norwegian Navy which had recently put into service someexcellent new ships. As for himself, his fondest dream had come true. He had had some basic technical training and was accepted in the Air Force.

He noticed that we were gazing at his face and again he became self-conscious and boyish.

We broke up, and I went out into the night. Sverre's story had made it all live again. I could see Norway before me. The thunder of Niagara made the illusion more real.

I saw the land lying there, waiting. The mountains were already white. Autumn storms were singing through the forests. The woods glowed in brilliant colours and hoar frost lay on the fields in the early morning before the sun gained strength. Another winter was at the door, with starvation and cold.

This summer the people had been sure that help would come. The young men had used their fat rations to oil their hidden firearms. They took desperate chances in preparation and in sabotage. The finest flower of our youth lay in nameless graves or pined away behind barbed wire fences. Old people died without seeing the liberation come. The people worked as hard as ever, but now there was neither joy nor honour in their travail. In the blacked-out cities they waited as in a fever for the Day.

But there was the message that this young boy had carried from them, that they could take it, and that they knew that help would come when it was ready. The people at home trusted the leaders who now held the Destiny of Humanity in their hands.

We had always been a quiet people who had never shown much emotion. Even now, no one cried out. Not with despair but with impatient hope came the almost audible whisper, "How long must we wait?"

XIX   *Comrades in Arms*

BUT so far everything had gone wrong with the war. Often it was only sheer strength of will and conviction that kept us going rather than logical thinking. But after Dieppe, things began to look up. Most of the news was good. Again there was optimism and a great deal of wishful thinking.

The jovial old liftman in the office buildings had recaptured his pre-war cheerfulness.

"We feel as if we were going up and up, don't we, Sir? Another couple of stops and we shall be in Berlin."

The barber at the corner declared that at last we had old Schickelgruber by the nose. North Africa was only the soaping, so to speak, preparatory to the real shave, which was bound to come soon. "Another couple of hair cuts and you will be back in Norway," he said.

Even the grand director of an old-established undertaking firm who lived in our street began to believe that the real business had begun at last, although he was a pessimist, both by nature and profession. He had put on his coat and come over to the garden fence to have a chat. Nice little tit-bits we are getting from the Caucasus. More and more Japanese ships sent to the bottom. Rommel leaving his guns behind him and the Italians their freshly-cooked macaroni. The Nazis would not last much longer now—only the embalming remained to be done. I indicated that in my view it was not quite so certain as all that yet, and added that I did not believe in a cheap funeral.

"A very sound point of view," said the old gentleman, becoming still more excited. He had lived for ten years in a German district outside

Milwaukee. The Germans were bad losers, he said; never had bronze or heavy mounting put in their coffins. Even the Italians ran to better funerals. The old man and I found much in common.

It certainly would be a mistake to think that America expected a cheap war. Everywhere new factories and military constructions are springing up. The hum of motors in the air becomes daily more insistent. More and more young people are being called up, so that the war is making itself felt in the homes. Once or twice I was given the opportunity of visiting American training camps. They inspired confidence. The troops looked like an advertisement for physical training. The meals might have been served in a luxury hotel. "Only the finger bowls are missing," said the officer who showed me round.

To-day, in an old fort, dating back to the wars with the Indians, men are being trained for war under all possible conditions in accordance with latest methods. There was a special battalion of Norwegian-speaking American recruits. During the winter they were to be trained in ski-technique. The officers were delighted to show me round.

"We Americans are not fundamentally a warlike nation. We have to build up a new army every time we go to war. It is costly, I grant you, but on the other hand, we get the latest of everything. Our weapons, our food and our morale are all up-to-date!"

We walked through the tastefully furnished and comfortable mess rooms. In the recreation rooms, many of the boys were writing letters. And we had, of course, to see the kitchens and the new refrigerators. The atmosphere was friendly and cheerful. There was not much clicking of heels here.

When we reached the office department, one of the officers pointed to a big pile of stencilled papers.

"Just take a look at those excellent questionnaires," he said. "They are supposed to be the latest thing in applied psychology. The other day some folk from the University, in brand new uniforms, came down here to investigate the morale of the troops. To begin with, we thought the whole thing nonsense, but they obviously knew what they were about and the men seemed to enjoy the business. About 800 were picked out to answer these questions and groups of assistants were carefully chosen from the intelligence tests here last summer. For a whole day, rivers of ink flowed. The questions ranged over everything between heaven and earth; the exercise and training received at the camp; their opinion of the sergeant and the cook; whether coloured troops ought to have separate recreation rooms; the kind of radio programmes they would prefer if they had to spend months on duty in Iceland; whether the laundry at the camp was satisfactory; and what they did last Saturday night.

I glanced through the questionnaires. Altogether they made quite a book and one could certainly not complain about the frankness of the style. At the end of each question, several answers were set out, from which the soldiers had to select the right one. "Be careful not to put your name anywhere in this exercise," the soldiers were instructed. "This is not an examination, it is simply a means of finding out your tastes, as if you were being asked whether you preferred your egg boiled or fried."

I noted down some of the questions.

"How do you think that most of the N.C.O.'s you know have been selected for their jobs?"

> Because of bootlicking or intrigue?
> By pure chance?
> Because they have been long in the Army?
> Other reasons?

"Do you think that you have a fairly clear idea of what this war is about?"

> Yes, quite a clear idea.
> No, not a very clear idea.

"Do you think that you are a good soldier?"

> Yes, one of the best.
> Yes.
> No, not yet, but I shall be.
> No.

Other questions had to be answered by "better," "less," "about the same."

"Do you think you would like the Army better

> If you had more marching?
> If you had more active service?
> If you knew you were going to be sent overseas to fight—
>> the Japanese?
>> the Germans?
> If you knew that you would never be sent over-seas?"

I asked the officers what conclusions could be drawn from such questionnaires. They said that they did not know exactly. Doubtless there was someone down in Washington who was dealing with these matters and perhaps there was some sense in it. They had the impression that the soldiers had given fairly honest answers.

An older officer who had taken part in the first world war said that to him the whole atmosphere seemed different this time. There was in a way less outward enthusiasm, less glamour this time; at any rate, there had been more parades and singing last time. Perhaps it was rather early to say that the soldiers in this war had certain characteristics in common, at any rate as far as Americans were concerned, but it seemed to him that there was more individual sincerity, as if the war were a personal matter.

Everywhere was the feeling that the war would claim sacrifices from each individual, even if they were not immediately called upon. The towns competed with each other in patriotic efforts. The shopkeepers loyally opposed hoarding. The workers, each in their way, worked loyally for the war. This was not a capitalistic war. Now it was really America's business. Even the foreign elements in the country co-operated. There was no doubt that most of the German Americans hoped for a new freedom for the land of their forefathers through a military defeat.

"Swedish" America showed their sympathy by arranging a special collection for Norway, not for food and clothes, but for planes.

In "Norwegian" America there was intensive work for both countries. The collections for the airmen and the sailors were most popular, as were personal gifts and work rather than money. Many people knitted socks and mittens to be used during the reconquest of Norway. There were many committee meetings, but many pairs of shooting mittens too. It was essential that these should have two fingers and the instructions were the subject of many discussions.

It was, of course, quite true that the war must be carried on on many fronts and with all sorts of weapons, but personally I rather drew the line at knitting needles. I was becoming impatient.

At last I got a reply from the Norwegian Government in London telling me that I could enter the Forces over there. But the question of transport was difficult, so that I must come alone and leave my family behind me.

This time we had more time to get ready. Siri thought it all great fun. We heard her talking to the neighbour's children over the fence telling them that now her father was going off to shoot the Germans. She got so excited that she took an almost new piece of chewing gum out of her mouth and stuck it on the fence while she pointed to my rucksack which had been hung out to dry after it had been cleaned. There they could see for themselves her father's parachute which would be filled with bombs and other noisy things. So now the war would soon be over and she would be able to go home to Norway and play hopscotch on the beach with flat stones.

We interrupted this performance and brought the child in. She had to realize that her father would only be a single skinny little soldier who could not end the war alone.

"But why are you going there, Daddy?"

"Because we must all do our bit. You remember the big boy who used to bring the milk round in the morning? He has already gone and Evelyn's father has gone, too. He used to wear a white coat and look at your teeth."

"Then I am sorry for the Germans."

"You need not begin to be sorry for them yet. First of all we have to get back our own and all the other countries they have stolen and they have still plenty of guns to shoot with."

"You must promise me to duck as soon as ever the Germans begin shooting at you."

I promised.

It was impossible to get a seat in a plane, but at last I was given a berth on a Norwegian cargo boat. We were two Norwegian and an English passenger who finally drove down to the coast and set out into the darkness. Next morning, we were well out to sea and there were heavily laden ships and light eager little corvettes as far as the eye could reach. As early as the following night, we had an alarm. It caused amazingly little excitement. These sailors were used to having U-boats after them like sharks. They all wore waterproof suits, with their life belts underneath. It was awkward playing cards in a life-belt, but according to the regulations, they had to be worn all the time. We heard shots in the night and the explosion of depth charges, but otherwise nothing happened.

The great topic of conversation was whether we would arrive in time for Christmas or not. There were no lighted Christmas trees awaiting us, but it was a good subject for discussion. We arrived just before Christmas and there was quite a difficulty about getting down to London. The trains were packed with sleepy soldiers who knew how to make themselves comfortable except for their legs. We were back in the war again.

London itself seemed to be as little affected as any town could be. The changes which the war had brought about had already become habits. The foreign Governments in London had found their feet and were working smoothly as part of the whole. And the Norwegian Ministries seemed to function very much as they did in the old days. All Norwegian men and women were in Government employ, most of them in uniform. Old friends were the same as ever. Perhaps there were some of them whose hair had turned a little, but as a compensation, they had more stars on their collars. I was glad that I had arrived in London as a mere civilian, or the strain of greeting them might have been almost too much for me!

While I was waiting to attend a special military course I was sent to visit the Norwegian forces in Scotland where the various societies in the camps wanted new speakers for their meetings. They were very anxious to hear about America.

Most of our camps are situated near some small, lovely, very neat Scottish town. Headquarters are generally in a shooting lodge or castle, and Nissen huts are spread out in the park or in the nearest field.

It sounded very impressive to be told that accommodation had been arranged for me in a castle. And the effect was not lessened by the drive through the stately, wrought-iron gates with an animal on the top, generally a lion rampant. But once inside the castle, all one's democratic instincts were soothed by the respect one could not but feel for those who had once lived within these walls. But the constant feuds with other clans seemed reasonable, as one shivered in the draughty passages, if only to keep themselves warm.

The Nissen huts are not hothouses, either. They are often camouflaged outside to make them look like the air around them. The boys told me that the illusion is more obvious inside than out.

However, there is no real grumbling about the conditions. The men have a good time, the country around them is lovely and the Scotch people extremely friendly. But the time seems long, the third year for many of them. The news from home is inspiring, but not exactly reassuring.

I met friends everywhere from all parts of Norway. A young soldier who was detailed to show me the way to the next camp was a boy from Narvik. He was a schoolboy when I saw him last.

"Yes he had had a hard time getting out of Norway, but it would be easier to get back." He showed me the parachute mark on his sleeve—that meant seven jumps. When one had done fifteen, one was given one's badge.

"Doesn't it give you a creepy feeling, falling through the air?"

"It does, rather, especially the first time. You don't feel too good sitting there around the open hatch waiting for your turn to come. We jump alternately, one from each side, and at that moment you don't feel particularly confident in these mechanical contraptions. But when you are hurtling through the air with the wind whistling in your ears, you don't think of anything in particular until you feel the strings taughten, then you float comfortably down towards the green ground. The fields are green all the year round over here. It is worse to jump at night as you may land on a hard place. A friend of mine landed right on top of the sergeant. It would have been even better if it had been the Colonel."

The troops are still in good spirits and the morale is excellent. They say that this is nothing to boast about as long as whisky is so expensive and the Scottish girls so prim. But apparently they have a certain amount of success in this latter quarter, as there have been a number of marriages between Norwegian soldiers and Scotch girls and the age-long bands across the sea are growing in strength. Norwegian names are to be found everywhere up there. Open boats have crossed the sea before, but this time they come to seek protection.

In one of the Scottish Firths there is an entire colony of Norwegian fisher-folk and their families who came across the North Sea in their fishing smacks. The young people are in the Army and the older ones fish with nets in the estuary where there are cliffs and sea-birds like at home.

The relationship between the Scotch and Norwegian fishermen is excellent. The Norwegian fishermen told me that the Scotch people were so kind and could not do enough for their guests.

"After we had shown that we could look after ourselves," grunted a grand old fisherman from the West Coast of Norway, turning over his quid of tobacco thoughtfully. He looked like an old Viking and had arrived with his boat laden with fishing tackle and family.

"No, that is not true," said his wife. "They were kind from the very moment we arrived. And we must remember that in a way these are their waters and that we are fishing their fish. They have even taught us some of their tricks with bait for fine line fishing and that sort of thing."

Whereupon the old man, not to be outdone in generosity, admitted that perhaps the Scot was not such a miserly fellow after all, he was only thrifty. "I believe they have put about these Scotch stories themselves," he said, "to get a bit of free publicity."

"My husband means well," said his wife, "but he is a little difficult. He even complains that the fish here are not up to Norwegian standard."

"Next year, at any rate, we shall have Norwegian cod for Christmas," maintained the old man.

Yes, indeed, we are impatient guests. Even the Norwegian school children who go to the Norwegian school in Scotland ask when they will get home to Norway, and when things will be as they were before. They are the children of members of the Government, fisherfolk, sailors and soldiers. They, also, live in a castle, Drumtochty Castle, one of the loveliest in Scotland, in the midst of rolling, hilly country, within the protecting bosom of Mother Britain.

The castle itself is romantic enough, with a rheumatic family ghost and a storied past. But perhaps it has never been fuller of odd human stories than it is now. One of them is lively little Per who managed to smuggle himself out of Norway without troubling either the legal or illegal organizations. His father was obliged to leave Norway as he was "wanted" by the Germans. As the journey across the North Sea in the depth of winter in a small boat was not without its dangers, it was decided to leave the family behind. But when the boat was clear of land, a thin little figure popped up from under some tarpaulins on the deck. "It's only me, Dad. I wanted so badly to come too." It was too late now to turn back—and that is how little Per came to Great Britain. When the little refugee is asked whether it is he who was the stowaway, he answers cockily, "Do I look like one?"

We have also schools in London. Perhaps they are not quite so pleasant, but they are just as necessary. I go to one of them and there is much new knowledge taught there which we have to absorb in the minimum time. We learn to look at our country dispassionately from the outside. We learn how to storm our own mountains and valleys. We learn all about the organization and psychology of the armies of our Allies. Perhaps all these wartime schools are in reality preparing us for the future of Europe.

London! No city in the world is so full of soldiers and has so few parades. No town is so full of history and has so little pathos. Everything is taken as a matter of fact, everyone feels so quickly at home. There are too many people everywhere, but no crowds. People are friendly and helpful, without being officious. Queues form themselves when they are necessary and disband themselves when they are no longer needed.

"And so move up a little," as Billy Brown says in the Underground posters. He is not a very exciting individual, but one cannot help liking Billy Brown of London Town.

We were a small company of Norwegians who sheltered in a pub during one of London's recent raids. Not that we had any objection to sheltering in a pub, we had already toasted the British Army in another. The rain of shrapnel forced us in. There were plenty of customers there already, yet we all found room. The orchestra tuned up. The guns sounded splendid. It made it more difficult to talk, but easier to contact one another.

The cigarette smoke lay like a smoke screen over us all, but we soon discovered that we represented a good number of the United Nations and both sexes. We were not quite certain of a Polish 2nd Lieutenant; but a lighter showed up a pair of very red lips, and we found room for the lieutenant at the table.

An American Captain stood a round of drinks in honour of Casablanca. He was the highest in rank so it seemed natural that he should have the honour.

"And when it comes to Lend Lease, there is not much left for us others to say," added a little Dane who in some way or other had got himself included in the company.

"The Danes take nothing seriously," we said, "they have no dignity and are as pretty and as flat as their country."

"And you are certainly dignified enough and as haughty as your mountains."

We passed quickly on to other amiable remarks about each other's characteristics and peculiarities and we regrouped ourselves a little so that Fighting France should not take too many liberties with the Polish

Lieutenant. Lend Lease had a tendency to loosen our tongues and we became full of chat.

"But quiet-mannered old Britain, with her class distinctions, must say something," we shouted through the noise of the fireworks.

"We are doing our best," came the answer, "and actually at the moment we are not as quiet as all that. As for our class distinctions they are not particularly obvious just at present. Look at that little A.T.S. girl over there at the bar. Can you tell by looking at her whether she is the daughter of a duke or of the landlord of this pub?"

"She is skinny enough to be highly born," said one.

"No, she is the landlord's daughter, because she is drinking her whisky neat," said another.

"That's no indication," said the Pole knowingly.

"Let's change the subject," said the American.

"Well, now it's America's turn," we said. "You have too much money, and you are always boasting."

"Yes, we have perhaps a tendency to boast," admitted the Captain, thus taking the wind out of our sails. "We are a young nation and want to be reckoned with."

We tried to talk a little about the future and we had a kind of desultory conversation about it. The noise outside died down and the landlord told us it was closing time.

Outside it was as dark as the grave. We walked in small groups round those who had torches and went on with our conversation. We talked in English as we could not see who was who. None of us had many illusions. The war would not be over by to-morrow, nor would the Kingdom of Heaven descend on earth the following day. We were all going to fight together, each for his own country, but also for something we had in common.

We walked in darkness. It was impossible to see anything, but we knew we were heading in the right direction.

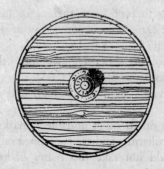